Relations

By the same author

MANY VOICES

WOMEN WRITING ABOUT MEN

SEDUCTIONS

MORE HAS MEANT WOMEN: THE
FEMINISATION OF SCHOOLING

SCHOOL FOR WOMEN

RELATIONS

Jane Miller

Jonathan Cape
London

Published by Jonathan Cape 2003

2 4 6 8 10 9 7 5 3 1

First published in Great Britain in 2003 by
Jonathan Cape
Random House, 20 Vauxhall Bridge Road, London SW1V 2SA

Random House Australia (Pty) Limited
20 Alfred Street, Milsons Point, Sydney,
New South Wales 2061, Australia

Random House New Zealand Limited
18 Poland Road, Glenfield,
Auckland 10, New Zealand

Random House South Africa (Pty) Limited
Endulini, 5a Jubilee Road, Parktown 2193, South Africa

The Random House Group Limited Reg. No. 954009
www.randomhouse.co.uk

A CIP catalogue record for this book is available from the British Library

ISBN 0–224–06391–X

Papers used by Random House are natural,
recyclable products made from wood grown in sustainable forests;
the manufacturing processes conform to the environmental
regulations of the country of origin

Typeset by Palimpsest Book Production Limited
Polmont, Stirlingshire
Printed and bound in Great Britain by
Biddles Ltd, Guildford and King's Lynn

For Karl, with love and thanks

Contents

Portrait of an Artist

Western Avenue, the A40, is one of several trunk roads out of London that were built during the twenties and thirties. Eventually, it takes you to Oxford. According to Nikolaus Pevsner, the historian of England's buildings, who often sounds murderous, it slices through and splits North-West London. The most recently revised Pevsner still gives more space to the remnants of old villages, a few mostly nineteenth-century churches and the occasional stately home lurking behind its kerbs and shoulders than to the industrial buildings barnacling this strip of 'Metroland'. Nor does Pevsner have much to say about the fenced-off rows of demolished houses or the oxblood boarding wrapped round the few remaining 'homes for heroes' promised by Lloyd George after the Great War, which once lined the road uninterruptedly from Shepherd's Bush to Gipsy Corner. For thirty years there have been plans to widen the road, and thousands of 'statutory instruments', evictions, wrecking balls and sledgehammers have done their worst. The Labour government dropped these plans the moment they came to power in 1997.

Bridget Cherry is now officially co-author of *London 3: North West* with Nikolaus Pevsner. He died in 1983, and she is anxious to 'update' him. She quotes as something of a period piece his 1951 verdict on the road's star attraction, the Hoover Building: 'perhaps the most offensive of the modernistic atrocities along this road of typical bypass factories'. It was famously designed to be appreciated from a passing car rather than from some static vantage point. Osbert Lancaster coined 'by-pass variegated' to describe the architectural style of the elaborately differentiated small houses leading to it. Nowadays, the 1933 building, once described as 'A Fairy Palace of Commerce', is admired again, for its gleaming whiteness, its grass-green window frames, and even for its 'art deco Egyptian motifs' and recessed stair towers, whose 'eye-catching quadrant-shaped corner windows with green glazing-bars have a distinct and perhaps not coincidental affinity with post-modern work of the 1980s'.

Twice a week I join the usually sluggish traffic on this arterial road in my bright blue Golf to visit my mother. She is almost ninety-two and has decided to lie on her bed fully and even brightly dressed for the rest of her life in the front upstairs room of the small semi-detached Victorian house my father bought, sight unseen, from an old friend in 1947. She wonders sometimes about going up in the new London Eye and even visiting the by now empty Millennium Dome, though these plans are complicated for her by the state of her 'innards'. When I suggest that she come downstairs, or even for a drive with me, she gives both options some thought, but usually replies more or less as she did last week, 'I can't say that I have an overriding desire to do either.' Occasionally she consents to a drive, and then she congratulates me on the light and on the beauty or the bareness of the trees, though she is always sad to see so few people about, as if she remembers a time when they would have been making merry before her very eyes. She would be the first to reject the idea that she has any right to the 'Wonderful, wonderful . . .' so carelessly bestowed on the old these days.

Still on the A40, I flash past the Hoover Building (no longer a factory, but the headquarters of a supermarket chain), getting exactly the fleeting sight of it that it was designed to provide, and turn right further on at the Polish war memorial, remembering the Polish generals who arrived at the end of the war in the street next to our house, where they remained, like their government in exile, 'in perpetual session', as a friend once put it, while their wives kept body and soul together mending nylon stockings at 6d a ladder in the dim light of their front rooms. I drive past the RAF base at Northolt and the cryptic signs to 'Northwood Headquarters' (the UK headquarters of NATO is a few miles north of here). I bump over the little railway bridge and the cutting that reminds me of Pissarro's *Penge Station, Upper Norwood*, as it once reminded my mother.

She lives at the distinctly 'lower' end of her late Victorian suburb (it is a characteristically Pevsnerian aperçu that all London suburbs had such ends), in one of the curving streets of small red-brick houses huddling round its two ugly churches and its railway station. My mother's house stands out, for it has been painted by a grandson in the palest peppermint with a faded cornflower-blue door and perhaps some thought of Pissarro. I have had glimpses of little tongues and loops of countryside on my way here, precious but deluding, more likely to lead to golf courses or sports grounds for workers in now defunct businesses than to farms or copses. There is a home for old actors in a flint-faced lodge, and I have seen the oldest and thinnest of its residents setting off at around three in the afternoon for his daily jog. This whole area must once have been hilly and covered in trees. You can tell from the gardens.

My mother has never quite fitted in. She knows this, though she puts it differently: that she always wanted to be in the middle of things and never was. She tells me that she was never clever enough for her mother, never as 'rapturously' Jewish as she grew up feeling she ought to be, then hopelessly in love with Henry Tonks who ran the Slade School of Art when she went there in the late 1920s at the age of seventeen, but never raffish enough for him. The man she married, she thinks now, was rather like him, except that Tonks had eyes that were 'a sort of nothing colour'. A fellow student, who became one of a small group of her male contemporaries to form what was sometimes called the Euston Road School in the late 1930s, was in love with her (though she feels that it's cheek to say so, even now). But 'I loved Tonks, and I think he guessed,' she admits ruefully. As a student she lodged with her best friend, Brynhild, in the Chelsea house of two 'loose' young sisters her brothers liked, round the corner from Tonks, as it happens. She still remembers that, and that he sent a telegram to tell her to come at once when he first saw her portfolio, but she couldn't live up to his expectations. She tells me now that the story about Tonks and his telegram was probably a joke, or at any rate a 'semi-joke'. The scholarship she was offered was swiftly withdrawn when her father wrote to Tonks suggesting it should be given instead to a student who needed the money. She spent long hours drawing from the model, and can still hear Tonks delivering his injunction to do some work every day of your life as he surveyed his students from his eyrie high up on the studio wall. She painted a few large biblical scenes at the Slade as well, a little like Rembrandt, though perhaps more like Ardizzone. Years later, I made a house for myself out of some of them and set a candle on a saucer inside to crown my labours. I don't think it occurred to my mother to blame me for the fire that destroyed the attic rooms of the house we lived in then, and her student oeuvre.

She thinks of herself as a lifelong depressive. I think of her as crippled by self-consciousness and given over to her disappointments, great and small. Yet she has also possessed an unusual will to survive what have sometimes been felt as torments. We talk now as we have rarely done before. She forgets our conversations almost at once, as she forgets my visits, my sisters' visits, and almost everything that has happened even that morning, and during the last week. When her sister or I suggest that she write things down in a notebook to help her remember them she tells us she has no time. She answers my questions, nonetheless, clearly and with sardonic brevity. Her concern is not with whether I should ask such questions or she answer them, but with whether she remembers things. She practises aloud for me walking round the house and garden where she grew up: the long curving drive, her mother's wood and garden, the fishpond with a lead tank in the middle. She remembers the rose garden and how you could just see it out of the window in the servants' hall through the gap in the tall, clipped hedge surrounding it; and then the walk to the engine room and down towards the orchard and the greenhouse and the field full of daffodils beyond that. She remembers the nursery wing, added by her father before she was born, balanced on an airy brick loggia and separated from the older parts of the house by the kitchens and the maids' bedrooms; and his secretary Miss Hagger sitting in a swivel chair in her office by the library. She visits the cottage where Miss Hagger lived with the head gardener when they married, and the pond where he drowned kittens in a sack. She describes her imaginary walk round all this with breathless pride only in her capacity to visualise it still. She felt as 'out of it' in her pretty, opulent home as she has felt ever since, and yet losing her memory, she says, is the worst of her losses.

When I arrive I make her a cup of tea. Her kitchen is cold and bleak and almost unchanged since the day she and my father moved in here with their three daughters. Neither of them cared about the look or the comfort of their houses or their clothes, though they cared about pictures. My father cared about painters and their fluctuating reputations more than their pictures, I sometimes thought. My mother cared about making pictures out of what she saw through windows, in streets and gardens, in hospital waiting rooms and parks and train carriages, and she cared about what she saw in her head. She still does. Lying on her bed in that upstairs room, in a nest of crumbs and scattered pages of the *Independent* (she has always wanted to want to read the newspaper, and the daily wreckage testifies to this), she draws on most days still, using crayons. These may be family scenes, with a sturdy woman in her forties dreamily in charge of a group of restless children, who seem to be playing Monopoly or gently quarrelling. Today she showed me a picture she had just done of two girls on a climbing frame, yet she had forgotten the story I'd told her which had probably inspired it. When one of my sons comes with me he searches the house for books he wants. His surreptitious removal of Herzen's *Memoirs* was wordlessly recorded by my mother in a sketch of a young man with knees raised high as he skips uneasily down the stairs in guilty haste, laden with books. She is no longer robust, as she once was, but bent and skeletally thin.

When my mother is gloomy she wonders whether she was right to be an artist. Was it sensible? As she looks at her own paintings on the walls of her room she can only find fault with them and is determined to work on their blemishes when she's feeling stronger. 'I've always thought I should be doing something I wasn't doing,' she explains. 'I have the makings of an unboring person, but in fact I am horribly boring and I must do better.' Should she change direction, jobs? I ask her what alternatives there were and are; she doesn't seem cut out to be an engineer or town planner. 'Being nice to people, I suppose. Educating myself. It must be wonderful to be paid for what you do,' she adds, in what I take to be a reference to her daughters' venality. I ask her what else she's been thinking about these last days, especially on Monday, when she had no visitors. 'Oh, a bit of this and a bit of that. Monday was a sort of dead day. Quite a good thing, really.' When I ask her questions about her parents she is more forthcoming. 'I adored my mum. But I don't think she was so keen on me. She was amazing, and I was rather a hopeless child, a bit flabby for her. I was probably insensitive. I was always unhappy, never able to accept things or other people as they were. Mum certainly wasn't very cuddly or easy to talk to; but she was an important person in the Jewish community. She translated the prayer book. She was rather grand, more so than my dad really, and formidable. And

very Jewish. She wasn't interested in art or music or dancing. I suppose my dad overestimated my talent.'

That was when she told me that though she felt at home in a synagogue, she never felt rapturously Jewish. Nor did her father, I suspect, not rapturously. Redcliffe Salaman was a doctor and a scientist, eventually the author of a book called *The History and Social Influence of the Potato* (for some reason, my mother has the Portuguese edition of it by her bed), who clearly needed to find a way of involving himself in the Jewish community, only partly for his wife's sake. At the end of his life, in the 1950s, he caused a stink among British Jews for advising them to abandon traditional Jewish methods of slaughtering animals. Until that moment he had seemed able to reconcile his agnosticism with his role as perhaps 'the last of the Anglo-Jewish notables', as the American historian Todd Endelman has described him. Curiously, none of his thirteen brothers and sisters was anything like as committed as he became to Jewish issues, nor were they as well educated or successful in what they did in the other bits of their lives. One of his brothers achieved fame in the family for owning a telephone at a time when so few other people did that he could only talk to the girl at the exchange. Another was the original owner of Augustus John's caravan and the payer of the painter's bills. These brothers did not get on together especially well.

I imagine there must have been a good deal of well-mannered tension too between my self-confident, rational grandfather and his dark and passionate wife, Nina. No doubt she missed London and the scholarly Jewish world in which she had made a name for herself. She seems to have turned away somewhat from most of her Derby family, who had repudiated Judaism, and devoted herself thereafter to Jewishness and, particularly, to Hebrew studies, supported in this by her father. It is true that she involved herself in the Women's Institute in the village after her marriage and that she and her husband paid for the building of its blue wooden hall, where their photographs presided damply in an upstairs room. My grandfather built his wife a tiny copper tower in which to write her poems while listening to the gurgle of the water tank; and a kosher chicken arrived forlornly each week from London in this rural paradise, where mornings began so exuberantly, I remember, with

the Gentile crowing of cocks. The front door of the
house where they lived near Cambridge – to which my
grandfather drove each day to run a phytopathology lab
for many years – opened straight into a sunny, spacious
hallway hung with paintings by the minor Pre-
Raphaelite painters Abraham and Simeon Solomon and
their cousin Solomon J. Solomon (who, it is said, added
the J to distinguish himself from his reprobate cousin,
Simeon). All three were my grandfather's relations, and
my mother didn't like any of their pictures much, though
she inherited one or two. Nor did she enjoy her Hebrew
lessons with her mother in the alcove under the panelled
staircase. She hated her governesses and manoeuvred to
get one of them sacked. Her brothers' tutors were another
matter.

Edward Platt, a young journalist, has published a book
called *Leadville: A Biography of the A40*, which made a bit
of a stir. My recent journeys have been enriched, if
imperilled, by my wanting to refer to his book as I drive
westwards, to pin down the house the squatters moved
into, and the one that is said to be full of Gypsies. There
is the block of flats on the other side of the road, whose
inhabitants remember better days and talk of 'former
glory'. The word 'decline' recurs again and again, vari-
ously inflected, in the conversations Platt has with
owners, tenants, squatters, professional protestors, offi-
cials: the decline of gardens, houses, cars, whole areas
and their 'tone' and 'class'. The environment, govern-
ments, life itself, all in decline: a coincidence, a harmony,
a Niagara of decline. Rats, real as well as metaphorical
ones, have taken over, and the foxes have moved on and
into London proper. One was found recently in the
House of Lords.

Neither of my parents learned to drive until their children had left home. They each took the driving test five times or more, and neither was ever easy at the wheel. They used to travel by train on the Metropolitan Line to Baker Street, and so did we. The trains had no corridors, and the carriages were sealed off from help or rescue until you reached the next station: Wembley Park, Neasden, Dollis Hill, Finchley Road were the counterparts of those rustically named roundabouts I pass through nowadays. Sometimes you wondered whether you would have to jump out of the train and on to the railway line. I remember two men communicating in sign language with exaggerated gestures and grimaces. I have never been sure whether they were deaf and dumb or faking it for effect. I almost jumped out on that occasion. My mother told me that she once sat next to Lady Diana Cooper, the famous beauty and actress, on that train. My mother introduced herself, and they had a rollicking chat. Rather late in the day, as usual, I took to reading difficult books on the train into London, in the hope, I suppose, of impressing some shy and serious male passenger, but I don't remember anyone enquiring about my reading matter. We didn't know much about Western Avenue in those days, only the railway line and its stations, most of them built in the late 1880s, some time after 1871, when Camille Pissarro was living miles away in South London and painting pictures of Penge station and the other sights of Upper Norwood. Wembley for us was not football, unforgivably, but a station and an accent, a kind of English, for my father was not indulgent towards those who spoke with what he called a 'Wembley accent'.

My mother says she knew my father 'only vaguely'

when she was at the Slade. Robert Collet had been at Bedales, as she had, though he was three years older and unlikely, as she puts it now, 'to come down to my level'. He was quite famous at the school, which is the oldest of England's co-educational boarding schools, for passing maths and getting his Matric, a qualification the school's headmaster thought something of 'a fetish', which did 'serious harm to education' and smacked of worldliness and ambition. Years later, my father went back to Bedales to teach the piano. He did two stints there, in fact. Ruth Salaman, on the other hand, my mother, took no exams and is sure she wouldn't have passed them if she had. One or other of her brothers had brought this dark-haired, blue-eyed prodigy to stay, and he had played the piano in the nursery 'so beautifully'. Only Miss Hartog, who taught them all the piano, played on it much and it was usually out of tune. My mother thought of my father then as 'a wonderful new discovery', who was simultaneously familiar and connected. 'A cathedral' is how he had seemed to her in those days. But, she tells me now, 'I was never in love with him. Or perhaps I was sometimes.' They went to Paris to get married when they thought she was pregnant. It was a false alarm, but by then they were married anyway. He wasn't Jewish.

Her mother had been dead for six or seven years by that time, and her father had remarried. Her brothers and sister did not welcome their new stepmother, but my mother quite liked her: a breath of fresh air, she says, who knew about London and artists, had worked as a photographer with the Italian Army in the First World War and briefly gone to prison with her sisters for suffragette activities. My grandfather built the tennis court for her, but for some reason she never played on it. Nor

I think did anyone else. I remember it as overgrown with blackberries, large, ripe ones. 'She was a bit anti-intellectual,' I point out. 'I know,' my mother replies, 'it was such a relief.' She let my mother cut off her pale yellow ropes of hair. My mother has always warmed to fellow outsiders, and her stepmother's discomforts and uncertainties may have chimed with her own. Her 'Well, here we all are, I suppose', pronounced with anxious formality at a family gathering, expressed all too well her shaken sense of the place she occupied there; and her 'I just love Proust. Sends little shivers up and down your spine' is remembered with some surprise. Could she, perhaps, have meant Poe?

The trouble was that my mother's father really minded terribly about her marrying a non-Jew and never quite forgave her for it. There were some grand Jewish families in London who 'showed her the door'. But my father could never see what the problem was. His family didn't in the least mind his marrying a Jew. They were just rather shocked that she knew so little about Judaism or even about her own family's history. Religions, as it happened, were one of their specialities. His aunt Clara thought of my mother as 'empty-headed' and used to send her letters back with the spelling mistakes corrected in red, and she returned my mother's Christmas presents to her without even bothering to open them, on the grounds of my mother's extravagance and foolish adherence to ritual. I always hoped that Clara got round to reading my mother's letters as well as correcting them, because she was a wonderfully funny writer at times, and Clara could have done with a laugh.

In Paris, my parents lived in a flat near the Parc Montsouris, though they returned to London for a month or two for my birth and then went back. My mother remembers that an old woman used to take me for walks in the pram. It wasn't the concierge, though, because she was known to give Calvados to babies who cried in the night. My parents were students in Paris. My father was studying the piano, with Isidore Philipp, and my mother went to classes taught by the printmaker Stanley William Hayter. The painter Gwen John met this young couple with their baby in Paris and marvelled in a letter home at these students who managed to look after a baby all on their own.

Between Hanger Lane and the turning off to the right at the Polish war memorial there are bits of landscape, though they are flat and swampy. Saplings have been planted by the roadside in lime-green plastic tubes. The refugees from Kosovo (asylum seekers, as they're now known) who sell grey roses, ramrod thin and sinisterly cloned, to motorists sitting in their traffic jams, give up at about this point. There are moments when you can imagine that some tired official from what is now grandly called the Department of Environment, Transport and the Regions might have been flown to the US – the one perk of a life's work, I dare say – to examine the parkways there and the lessons to be learned from Robert Moses's road-building in the 1930s. In the summer the scrub on both sides of the road is hidden by wild flowers. There used to be a few patchwork allotments, where men (for the most part) grew vegetables and then sat among them on upturned boxes having a smoke. My mother often painted allotments. In the long list of men she has doted on since Henry Tonks, gardeners predominate. Driving instructors were also favoured for a while. My earliest memory of a man 'Mum's got a pash on' is of our next-door neighbour, a town clerk and dedicated gardener of exceptionally few words, who later wrote her stumbling and affectionate letters, no doubt in response to more practised ones from her. He sometimes enclosed snaps of himself with his wife and two children, perhaps as a reminder.

My mother's paintings are full of rosy-cheeked artisans taking it easy. Even when they are up ladders and on roofs, they are not as a rule very strenuously occupied. For a long time she went to the canal a mile or two away from home to draw and paint the boats and barges, the towpath and the locks and the willows. Her pictures glow with romance and a bucolic innocence she has invented for herself, but which she recognises and cherishes when she finds it in other people. *Le Grand Meaulnes* was her favourite book for years, and she loved Samuel Palmer's work. She has thought of Iris Murdoch and Barbara Pym as having some of this carnival quality while also being 'down to earth'. She can rarely, if ever, have drunk in a pub or watched a football match, yet in her pictures charming young men laugh together over a pint and tangle on football fields, as well as stooping to their leeks and potatoes. Her own exclusion from such scenes must have constituted a good deal of their glamour, and she was always convinced that working-class people were nicer and better at family life than anyone she knew.

Taken to task by a teacher years ago for hanging about at lunchtime, my younger sister explained that there was 'not much point in going home as Mum is catching the autumn'. She has always been best at gardens and inhabited landscape, sometimes magically so, and there are usually buildings somewhere in her paintings, and people, happy, preoccupied, utterly sure of themselves: their importance to themselves and the world unquestioned. Her hundreds of linocuts illustrating Old Testament stories manage to domesticate and mythologise their scenes at the same time. Raw nature, on the other hand – sunsets and mountains and seas – was never her thing, nor were spring and summer, seasons of depression. Sometimes there are women in her pictures, bundled up against the cold, housewives. I don't think she sees herself as one of them.

A cousin has sent me photographs of my mother as a girl. She is enchanting in them: dancing, posing, laughing, deep in high summer grass and pretty as a picture. I show them to her and tax her with looking happy in them, undeniably (and unendurably) happy. 'Well, I liked showing off,' she admits crossly, 'doing what I liked doing.' As well as singing and dancing, falling in love was the main thing she liked doing. At school it was a matter of who was 'keen' on whom. It still is. She tells me that being in love is a cure for depression, even when it is unrequited. She would like me to divulge secrets, love affairs. I have been a disappointment to her in this respect and in others. Her three daughters belong in her category of 'ordinary people', non-artists, fitters-in, good at unimportant things like driving cars, using computers and tidying up. And it is true that when I've tried to characterise my mother for someone who doesn't know her, 'incompetent' is one of the first words that come to mind, though it is not the right one. She knows and regrets that there are no secrets to be prised out of me and falls back on what she imagines will be more fruitful topics: how I got on with my father, for example, her

husband of sixty-one years. I tell her carefully that there was a time when I felt put down by him and his lofty incorruptibility, which could make you feel trivial. And then, when I told him I'd been reading something – say Balzac's *La Peau de chagrin* – he wouldn't talk about it, ask what you thought, he'd just recommend that you read *Illusions perdues*. And he could never understand why his daughters might need, let alone want, more than one pair of shoes. 'How many feet have you got?' he would ask, with biting jocularity. I think we got on well, though, if not intimately. I was proud of his cleverness and good looks, but maddened by his certainties and his particular brand of deafness.

I suddenly remember a linocut my mother made of him. He is concentrating on looking at a painting in an exhibition, while a small girl (I think of her as me, but she is probably a granddaughter) is tugging furiously at his hand to come and look at something else. 'He could be rather distant, dry,' I say, 'couldn't he?' My mother's sketches of her dry, gifted husband have often been slyly comic and extraordinarily like him. There is a funny wood engraving of him playing the bassoon. Ridicule was all his wife and daughters had to hand at times. He did not play the bassoon very well, and it didn't suit him, despite – or perhaps because of – his scholarly range and fastidiousness as a musician. But 'dry' doesn't do justice to his ambition or his integrity as a concert pianist. I was moved and a bit ashamed all over again when I read the other day what he wrote in 1958 about the playing and the teaching of the pianist Vlado Perlemuter, whom he came to know. He starts by remembering a conversation he once had with his own old teacher, Philipp, who was ninety-five by then:

He mentioned Perlemuter as a man whom he greatly admired, and said I was to remember the name and be sure to take any opportunity I had of hearing him. I remember in particular his saying 'Il joue avec simplicité', which I think was what Philipp felt was the quality most lacking in so many pianists today – the gift of reacting spontaneously to the work, so that the personality of the interpreter serves to transmit, possibly to enhance, but never to distort whatever it is he may be playing. What struck me at once about Perlemuter was this selflessness in his approach to the music. It is easy to say that of course this should be the attitude of all true interpreters; in fact it requires most unusual qualities of sensitiveness and understanding if the result is not to be a merely negative lack of personality.

Mostly, my father is reading a book in my mother's drawings of him, with a slightly disdainful air: a man at once deep in a book, but also detached from it.

'Well,' my mother replies, gathering her energies, 'he was homosexual. Perhaps that's why you thought him dry. Though I don't think he was completely, only, homosexual. He liked girls when he was younger. Diana and Karen somebody or other and that singer called Jennifer.' She has told me these things before and I know she expects something from me in response, although I don't think either of us knows what it is. Should I ask her what the connection is, in her view, between dryness and homosexuality, or how (indeed whether) his being homosexual mattered to her, or indeed to me? It presumably mattered a good deal to him. 'Is it true that he

ran off with that girl, that friend of yours from the Slade?'
I ask instead, evasively and in order to deflect her and
see what she'll say, since the story about the two run-
aways getting as far as Le Puy, before my grandfather
somehow persuaded them to return, is an old one, with
ramifications. Apparently, it wasn't the only time that this
particular lady made off with a friend of the family, and
she came from a family of bolters. My mother remembers her affectionately, even though 'she did me in'.

I've more or less known that my father had homosexual sympathies since he lent me André Gide's *Corydon*
when I was seventeen and laughed when I asked him
afterwards what could have possessed him to do so. If
he had an active homosexual life, he didn't talk about
it to any of us, and I assumed in those days that it was
either some kind of literary fantasy or that it wasn't and
he didn't want us to know of its existence. Perhaps he
thought we would be shocked or disapproving. I ask my
mother whether they ever discussed these things. 'Not
really,' she says, 'but he knew I knew.' She has never said
that she minded exactly or even found it difficult, though
she attributes the fact that there were 'no cosy chats or
anything' in their marriage to his homosexuality. 'It was
probably a bore for him. It was certainly a bore for me.
But then I've always been a bit homosexual too.' This
time I am surprised. 'Yes,' she goes on, 'I was in love
with Eileen for about two years, but she was in love with
Isolde.'

The solid, high green fence is meant to disguise the
absence of all those houses along the motorway that
were pulled down for nothing. There is total stalemate
now: widen roads and you encourage motorists. Public
transport, however, is near collapse in London; and the

man who 'turned round' the New York and Boston subway systems has been imported to bring order to our Underground. Western Avenue boasts its spanking-new car showrooms, computer warehouses and 'self-storage' depots (I think of them as neatly filled by a hundred raging agoraphobes), but the few houses left are 'trashed, rehabbed and squatted', in the words of an inhabitant who should know. Much is made these days of what pollsters call 'the pebble-dash vote'. 'Pebble-dash' is that particularly rough and rebarbative stucco applied to many 1930s houses and guaranteed to tear savagely at any hand laid lightly upon it. The same houses and the same people living in them were simultaneously hailed and sneered at in the thirties. They still are. But then there is a letter in the newspaper today from an inhabitant of Penge, who ends her defence of that much older suburb with the line, 'Go and snigger in Notting Hill.' J. B. Priestley called these new suburbs 'essentially democratic', 'an England, at last, without privilege', and George Orwell did too, though he shuddered at 'the newness of everything! The raw, mean look! The kind of chilliness, the bright red brick everywhere . . .'

On my mother's ninety-first birthday, my sister and I brought whisky and asparagus and some of our grandchildren to see her. The presents, once they'd been exclaimed over, slipped down the side of her bed. I am reminded of the time when I gave my parents a typescript copy of a book I'd written. Like so much else, it fell and scattered irretrievably beneath my mother's bed. 'I suppose it doesn't matter terribly, does it, what order the pages are in?' she asked. On her birthday, one of her great-granddaughters did her portrait, starting from her feet and taking particular trouble with the lozenges of colour on her blanket. My mother worried that all the people who weren't there, hadn't been asked, might take offence. 'I really ought to do something, have a party,' she told us more than once as we tried to entertain her. Her private images of fun and human intercourse have always won out over the real thing.

Recently, she has taken to asking me about my memories of childhood, and sometimes I suspect her of angling for compliments or at any rate reassurance that it wasn't all too bad, that a childhood illness of mine, for instance, was not all her fault. I oblige, though half-heartedly. I'm not sure that she is in the mood to listen to cons as well as pros. Sometimes she insists, with gusto, that at least the two of them must have got something right, if only through their genetic difference from one another: 'After all, there isn't a single idiot in the family.'

Edward Platt quotes Lloyd George, who thought of 'the money spent on houses as an insurance against "Bolshevism and Revolution"'. He regarded the new houses, 'each with its own garden, surrounded by trees and hedges, and equipped internally with the amenities of a middle-class home', as providing 'visible proof of the irrelevance of revolution'. Now the squatters along the motorway have run whole rows of back gardens together into communal ones. The engaging individuality of those pairs of houses, and the subtly maintained distinctions between council-owned property and owner-occupiers, have dissolved and disappeared. There are sale signs up for developers to take over from now on. It is the twenty-first century and no one is waiting for a miracle or a revolution.

As I drive back along the motorway to London in the evening I think of Auden's lines in memory of Yeats:

> Silence invaded the suburbs,
> The current of his feeling failed . . .

Today my mother's arm has been hurting her quite badly, making the performance of her bodily functions more difficult than ever. 'Other people seem to know how to end their lives, do away with themselves,' she points out as I struggle to lift her back on to her bed, 'but I don't.' Even decline and death are secrets withheld from her, something other people manage with enviable ease behind her back, another bit of life people seem always to have known about and never divulged.

The Potato Man

My grandfather wore beautiful clothes: heavy silk jackets, dark red or green, pale sandy-coloured tweed plus-fours and shoes as glossy as chestnuts. When he went to London he looked like Winston Churchill, only better, because his silky white hair, once red, curled out beneath the brim of his black homburg, whereas you always knew that Churchill hadn't any hair to speak of under his. I suppose my grandfather was rather a flashy dresser, with his looping gold watch chain and wide wedding ring, his flannel waistcoats, his hand-knitted socks with their cable-stitch turnovers, his bow ties.

I don't imagine my grandchildren will remember my clothes with such pleasure. They may believe, as I believed, that acquiring clothes is something the old do naturally, without thought. It would have been difficult to imagine my grandfather in a shop or a tailor's: his clothes were too much a part of him for that. None of them looked new or likely to have occasioned him that mixture of self-consciousness and pleasure that wearing something for the first time can give you. In fact, it turns out, he thought about clothes a good deal. One of those flannel waistcoats, now on its way to the wardrobe of a great-great-granddaughter, was announced in a letter to his wife as 'something I shall like and you always admire'; and when once she contemplated buying a fur coat, he replied by the next post, 'I should

be frightened of it, my dear, to say nothing of not being able to afford it.'

He was undeniably a patriarch, though he did better as a grandfather than a father. It was felt that there were favourites among his six children, and they had memories of being fussily dressed up to visit their parents for half an hour or so in the library after tea: an oddly Victorian practice for someone so keen on modernity, but he had memories of seeing his own father no more than once a week when he was a child. He told his daughters at crucial moments that they'd broken his heart, and there was resistance among both the girls and the boys to what were thought of as unrealistic expectations (low ones as well as high). And then his search for a second wife so soon after the death of his much loved first one was regarded by some as precipitate, and as hardly excused or explained by the need for someone to take charge of his two young daughters. Yet my sisters and I still have letters he wrote to us as children, which are funny, generous, teasing and marked by his sense of the differences among us; and I know that most of his fourteen other grandchildren felt about him as we did. He believed in praising the young – often against our parents' better judgement – and was protective of us, and also, especially so, of my mother, the older of his two daughters. I once lay screaming for her in a small bedroom in my grandfather's house, far from the dining room where the grown-ups were eating. There was an engraving of Alexander Pope above my head and linen curtains at the window, swarming with birds perched back to back on little branches. I was screaming for the hell of it and loudly, oddly certain that no one could hear me but my mother. When my grandfather appeared and told me quietly never, ever to disturb my mother again during dinner I froze with shame. Later, when I was fourteen, he summoned me to the Athenaeum to rebuke me for an outburst of rudeness reported to him by his daughter. I remember sitting on a bench in the club's main hallway – women and girls were not allowed beyond that point – and watching the bishops go by in their gaiters as my grandfather alluded cryptically to what he saw as my mother's problems. 'You can't make an omelette,' he said, 'without breaking eggs.'

My father was implicated in that dud omelette, though I was not sure why or how in those days. Whatever it was might have explained the chilliness between these two admirable men, who were never anything but civil to one another, though my father snarled a few of his true feelings for his father-in-law during the final unhappy months of his life. He resented the respect that had surrounded this man who had never needed to earn a living. For the story goes that my grandfather's father left each of his fourteen surviving children enough money in 1896 to live without working for the rest of their mostly long lives. My grandfather was number eight, born in 1874 and named Redcliffe after the London square where the family lived briefly and where he was born. An older brother had been named Euston on the same principle, and the family had moved west just after his birth, allegedly because a neighbour's cook had murdered her mistress and boiled the body in the scullery copper.

I am pretty sure that none of my grandfather's thirteen siblings ever did paid work, and even he writes of a working life that was more a matter of chance than of judicious choice, neither linked to payment. Myer, their father, the youngest of seven, inherited a thriving leghorn hat and ostrich feather business established in East London in 1816 by his father, Isaac, when the family name seems for no good reason to have been changed from Solomon to Salaman. My grandfather thought it was a signwriter's error. This family of Ashkenazi Jews had lived in England for about a century by that time and had prospered modestly as merchants. There was strong family and community feeling, but no tradition of piety or scholarship or indeed of anything in the least rabbinical. Myer expanded his father's business into property development in London, employing his somewhat feckless older brothers, and became a rich man. He first bought, and then elaborately rebuilt, a large house for his family in Mill Hill, where they spent six months of the year. The rest of the time they lived in the centre of London. It was from Mill Hill that Redcliffe (the first member of his family to take a public examination) rode on horseback to the London Hospital at the turn of the century, where he studied and then practised as a doctor and was later made director of its Pathological Institute.

In his preface to *The History and Social Influence of the Potato,* a book he was engaged in writing for most of the last twenty years of his life, and which was published in 1949, my grandfather wrote:

My career as a medical man and pathologist was brought by illness to a sudden close in 1903. Eight years had elapsed since I had left Cambridge: five strenuous and fruitful years had been passed in the laboratories and wards of the London Hospital, and three more in a ceaseless effort to find time for research after the heavy claims on my time as administrator and teacher had been satisfied.

In the following year, I retired to what prom- ised to be a life of ease and leisure in the beautiful village of Barley, in North Herts. In less than a couple of years my health was completely restored and I was able, once more, to lead a physically active life. Thirty-two years of age, happily married, free from financial cares, and devoted to hunting, one was unconsciously graduating for the part of a Jane Austen character. But I discovered, as I believe her men also would have done, had not their careers invariably terminated with their capture and mental sterilization at the altar, that 'respectability', even with a corresponding income, is not enough. It is not easy to identify, as one approaches the end of life's course, the motives which propelled one in any specific direction, in the days of one's early manhood. Not least was the fact that, whilst in the winter months I was sufficiently occupied with hunting, in the summer, having no liking for golf, tennis or cricket, I was at a loose end.

That gentleman amateur's voice persisted to the end of his life, and the paradox he has always embodied for me starts there. He hunted as a young man, but he also nearly died of TB, contracted as he delivered babies in the East End, and he told me once that at least five of his medical student contemporaries had died of untreated septic throats and that he had only survived TB because he could afford to eat properly. There had been an epidemic, which was neither admitted to nor contained, and young hospital doctors were grossly overworked, as they still are, and vulnerable to septicaemia, for which there was no cure. He remembered those years as the happiest of his life, nonetheless: 'Many a time I have been met with the invitation – "Will you have a cup of tea, doctor, or a drop of methylated?"' He began to learn about poverty and class, and much later he put to use what he had learned in his book about the potato.

When I knew him best he was a handsome, healthy man in his sixties and then seventies, and strikingly confident. I knew about adults who wept and sulked, longed for the impossible and regretted things: literature offered examples as well as life. My grandfather seemed to me altogether above all that: stoical, contented, tolerant and conciliatory by nature. His person, his house, his garden, his relations with everyone in the village where he lived in squirelike splendour until his death in 1955, beamed with assurance, harmony and a benign and intelligent curiosity. During the holidays, whole families, or groups of grandchildren of about the same age, would stay with him and his second wife, Gerts, or Gertie, and after tea he would take little parties of us on walks round 'the triangle', probably two or three miles at most of small roads linking three or four clusters of farms and cottages, and point with his stick as he told us stories, memories, the latest news: each household and every inch of the land known and remembered in their successive generations. He had farmed some of it himself in his youth. Once or twice we met his old friend James Parkes on our walks. Parkes was a clergyman and an authority on the relations between Christianity and Judaism, who lived in the village. We would wait in agonised impatience as the two men swiped the hedgerow with their sticks and talked for an hour at least.

I can still smell and feel in my lungs the sour, sooty fumes of the old LNER train leaving King's Cross for Royston (stopping at all stations to Cambridge, and I could list them). There were the orange tin plaques on the siding out of the station advertising Virol 'For Maids', which I found puzzling, and still do. On one occasion we made an effort to spread ourselves across a whole compartment so that my mother could feed the baby unwatched, and my father put on her hat and stood grinning inanely at the window with his hand on the punched leather strap that held it up, in an attempt to repel likely co-passengers. At Royston we could see the old grey Wolseley across the fence, sometimes with my grandfather at the wheel, more often with his driver, Stanley; and when we arrived and the car stopped under the May tree in front of the house, our step-grandmother would usher us with unseemly haste, as it appeared to us, into the downstairs cloakroom with its low-slung lavatory seat and footstool, designed and built in the early years of the twentieth century, according to some arcane theory of health and natural posture out of the palest oak.

I have never loved a house as much as that one, though it was a curious hotchpotch and not conventionally beautiful: one end early nineteenth century, with large elegant rooms, bow windows, panelling and fancy plaster ceilings; the bit in the middle constructed out of a sixteenth-century farmhouse, to which my grandfather had added a large nursery wing in about 1902; Edwardian and 'modern', I suppose, airy and sunny and painted white and perched above a brick loggia, where bikes and prams and deckchairs were kept and which I remember being blocked up with sandbags at the beginning of the war. Right at the top was the tiny copper tower, with its golden cockerel for a weather-vane, where my grandmother had been expected to write her poems. It was she, it turns out, who had discovered the house when her husband was ill and away convalescing. He had not thought he would live there for long.

My grandfather yearned for company and was always pleased to see us. It was easy to make him laugh until he cried and then watch him take off his glasses to wipe his eyes with an elegant and voluminous silk hand-kerchief. As my mother unpacked our suitcases, she could be counted on to spill talcum powder, or, on one occa-sion, a tube of white oil paint, which she ground firmly with her heel into the mossy green carpet of No. 4 bed-room, almost as if the carpet might be all the better for it. All the bedrooms were numbered, but from the begin-ning of the war the numbers above 5 or so – the ones in the nursery wing – were out of bounds, lived in first by twenty evacuees and later by the village rector and his wife. Gertie had jettisoned her tennis, her photog-raphy, her past as a suffragette and her lively London ways to run this country house and turn herself into a good wife; but she was never comfortable with any of it or with any of us, poor woman. There is a story that on her arrival there her new husband had invited her to do whatever she wanted to do, so long as she changed nothing in the house; and I don't think she did.

In summer, we would dash straight into the garden, to the swing dangling from a chestnut tree, to the dank

remnants of a moat, to the vast raspberry and goose-
berry frames and the Jerusalem Orchard planted and
named to celebrate the Balfour Declaration in 1917.
There, we would make ourselves sick on plums, or steal
into the greenhouse for the smallest, warmest, most delicious tomatoes in the world. My mother once complained that in her childhood it was her parents who
got the few artichokes or strawberries the gardener
brought into the house, but that by the time she was a
mother herself fashions had changed and the children
got the pick of everything. In winter, we would lie like
the sun's rays round a small art deco electric fire in the
library, our legs mottling, and read and read again the
Teddy Lester books, Angela Brazil, Louisa M. Alcott, *The
Fifth Form at Saint Dominic's*, P. G. Wodehouse, all left
there by our parents. We put on plays and danced to
Grieg's *Peer Gynt* and 'Our Miss Gibbs' Lancers' on the
wind-up gramophone, and the grown-ups were sometimes prevailed upon to watch us. We ate our meals with
the servants in the servants' hall until we were eight or
nine, and we could be kept there all afternoon by Gladys,
the cook, if we refused to finish our food. My grandfather housed 'his' refugees in the stables during the war,
and we would oblige him by visiting Dr Eschelbacher
there, who gave us Hebrew lessons, somewhat against
our will. Other refugees, an academic and his family
from Vienna, were given a cottage in the village among
'the peasants', as they crossly remembered it.

My grandfather could not be disturbed in the
morning. He would settle at the vast double desk, built
for him and his first wife by the village carpenter Mr
Chuck, dictating family and business letters and then
chapters of his book to Miss Hagger, who had grown

up above the village shop and post office and come to work for him when she was sixteen. It was said that the servants ran a book on who my grandfather would marry after his first wife died and that their money was on her. Had she been Jewish, he might well have married her, out of love and gratitude, for he relied on her for everything. She, more than anyone, understood the link between Jews and potatoes, which was, as she put it, that 'both involve problems of heredity'. Eventually, Miss Hagger married the head gardener, Martin Hayes, as his second wife. My grandfather wrote in a note attached to his will that some kind of memorial to the family might appropriately be placed in the village hall if only to remind disbelieving future generations of the excellent relations that had existed for more than half a century between this Jewish family and the inhabitants of a Hertfordshire village.

Explaining his loneliness as a boy, Redcliffe remembered himself as a prig and gave as an example his leaving Cambridge in 1896 before his fourth year (he already had a first in Natural Sciences) because his father had died and he was certain that he was the only one of the children capable of looking after his widowed mother. He also turned down an invitation in that year to take part in the famous Torres Straits expedition of 1898. He regretted both decisions, not least because he found that he was far from indispensable to a mother who saw to it that each of her seven daughters visited her daily in the Harley Street flat where she spent the last thirty years of her life. His disapproval of drinking and adultery (activities he believed to be statistically rare among Jews) had something of the prig about it too, though he comfortingly linked both statistics to Jews' better infant mortality and general longevity rates and their resistance to TB and womb cancer (advantages which had in their turn to be balanced against a Jewish tendency to flat feet and piles). I thought it priggish as well as unnecessary of him to warn me against young male members of the aristocracy when I was at university, on the grounds that they were unlikely to have brains or consciences. I remember meeting him unexpectedly on King's Parade in Cambridge, so that I was obliged to introduce my companion to him. There was no obvious recoil on my grandfather's part, however, from the charming young man in the Inverness cape, who, but for the grace of a Jewish or Catholic God, might so easily have been carrying a wholly disgraceful guitar and a brace of pheasants as well.

There were those, I know, who regarded my grand-father's confidence as arrogance and his apparent denial – or anyway absence – of any sense of contradiction as bluff or pride, a refusal to admit that the different aspects of himself might be thought to occasion friction. He was presumably joking when he wrote in a letter to Nina, his wife, that he thought of himself as 'a really charming example' of 'the Englishman of the Jewish persuasion'; but I think he regarded his lifelong sympathy with Zionism as perfectly compatible with his uncomplicated identification with a patrician England he was also able to blame passionately for most, if not all, of Ireland's famines and other catastrophes. He could call himself 'an amateur researcher', while undoubtedly thinking of himself as a trained and professional scientist who was proud to be elected a Fellow of the Royal Society in 1935. Yet he began and continued his researches into the potato and its varieties and diseases in his own large garden and in collaboration with his head gardener – though later he set up and ran the government-funded Potato Virus Research Station in Cambridge.

Out of his experimental work – raising potato seedlings by the thousand, studying their genetic make-up and searching for and eventually finding a variety that was immune to blight – he turned himself into a historian. He came to see that the potato, whether wild or cultivated, and whether grown and eaten in Peru in the sixteenth century or in Ireland or the Highlands of Scotland from the sixteenth to the nineteenth cen-turies, could shed light on particular forms and man-ifestations of poverty, and on the social arrangements that had produced them at different times and in dif-ferent places. The book that he wrote about this long and complex history of one of the world's essential foods, and the part it had played in simultaneously assuaging poverty and exacerbating it – 'for close on 300 years the potato both stabilized and perpetuated the misery of the Irish masses' – is a remarkable one, which absorbed him for a good deal of his later life. His publisher seriously considered submitting the book and its author for the Nobel Prize, in goodness knows what category, but the idea was dropped. It was widely and admiringly reviewed as a pioneering work of social and historical research, though it was barely discussed in Ireland – something that surprised and disappointed my grandfather and caused him to wonder whether Protestants controlled the newspapers there. The book, which is still in print in several languages, stands as a warning against the dangerous reductions and vulnerabilities that reliance on any single crop or food can produce. He writes with fury of 'this incredible drama of spite and imbecility' acted out in eighteenth-century Ireland and later, and of what was going on in England at the same time:

> The attitude of the older privileged class towards those they felt to be below them, was based on tradition and blessed by the Church. It was a kind of glorified selfishness, whose nakedness had been draped, and whose features adorned, by the refinements of what was probably the most cultured age in our history. The radical industrialist came with a different outfit. In him, selfishness, sublimated as a spirit of enterprise, reappeared on the social stage as a virtue, the possession of which was envied by the Established, sanctified by the Dissenting

Churches, and measured by both in terms commensurate with the bank balances of the virtuous. The corollary, that failure and poverty were evidence of darkness and sin, was inevitable.

Significantly, he writes of 'our history'. As a historian he is comfortably English, though his story entails criticism of the English. The scope and detail of the book's passionate historical narrative may be read as an attempt to integrate potentially centrifugal tendencies in his own life, and to rework ideas and theories he took from the eugenics movement of the early years of the twentieth century. There were ways in which these also underpinned his sympathy for Zionism, though they probably bore less ambiguous fruit eventually in his scientific researches into the genetics of potato varieties and the diseases they were prey to.

He was not yet a historian when he published *Palestine Reclaimed* in 1920 – a book that is often omitted from his curriculum vitae, perhaps out of tact – though he had already begun work as a scientific researcher when he wrote it and had published several papers under the benevolent eye of William Bateson, considered by one historian of eugenics, Daniel Kevles, to be 'the leading British Mendelian'. *Palestine Reclaimed* was a book put together from the letters Redcliffe wrote to his wife Nina from Egypt and then from Palestine during 1918 and 1919, while serving as Regimental Medical Officer to the 2nd Judean Battalion of the 39th Royal Fusiliers, and he scrupulously omitted from his book what I should have liked to read there: his intimate communication with his wife, questions about their five children and so on. One of their twin sons had died of pneumonia in

1913 and was to be remembered, as other lost children have been, as the cleverest of them all. All this is to be found, I have since discovered, in the archives he left to be housed by the nation, as are his wife's rather less ebullient letters to him.

The very existence of these papers in their thirty or so carefully labelled brown boxes reminds me of my dilemma in relation to this man and his life. He was, and he enjoyed being, a public figure, someone whose friends were likely to be 'distinguished', a word his grand-daughters were apt to treat with mirth; and his archive, which is sometimes visited by people who are not his grandchildren, contains testimonies to his forty-three years as a JP and magistrate in Hertfordshire, his work for the Jewish community in England and, during the Second World War, for Jewish refugees from Europe, his fellowship of the Royal Society, his governorship of the Hebrew University in Jerusalem, and his preoccupations and achievements as a scientist and as a writer. This public side to my grandfather distances him in some ways, makes him harder to decipher, but I have come to see that it also accounts for a sense, intermittently recognised by his children and grandchildren, that his ease in the world, his assurance, could seem to confer on us a precarious right to a place and a voice in the same world, sometimes against the odds. That is what patriarchs do for their families, their descendants, I suppose.

Those brown boxes also contain long passages of unpublished autobiography, written at the end of his life with the declared intention of going beyond or beneath his public self. This is an intention which is not fulfilled, as he seemed to acknowledge, though there are accounts of his childhood and his unhappiness at St Paul's School and then at Cambridge. In the middle of his enormous family he seems to have longed for an intimacy which he only achieved later, in his marriage to Nina Davis in 1901, perhaps with no one else, though he had important, lasting friendships from Cambridge onwards. He admits to murderous dreams about an older brother he doesn't name, and he was not close to his other brothers or to most of his sisters, though he became friends with two of his brothers-in-law: Fred Samuel, who figures in *Palestine Reclaimed* as a fellow army officer in Palestine, and Charles Seligman, who started life as a medical student, as Redcliffe did, and went on to become Professor of Ethnology at the London School of Economics and to correspond regularly with Redcliffe about their sometimes shared research interests, particularly in questions of race.

Redcliffe clearly admired his own father's energy and entrepreneurial boldness and his mother's humour, directness and capacity to run her teeming household without fuss; though her main achievement in his eyes was to have provided her children with 'the noblest of women as a Nurse'. It was to this nurse, Emily Hewitt, that he wrote from school, 'I am very unhappy and please spread it.' And it was she, he remembered, who imbued the Salaman children with their sense of superiority, by requiring servants to stand up in their presence and forbidding any truck with the children of the poor. Redcliffe's only slightly shamefaced admission chimes with my own sense of having also enjoyed some uncomfortable privileges, bestowed – if in less draconian ways – by him.

My grandfather arrived in Palestine less than a year after the Balfour Declaration, that short, momentous letter sent by the British Foreign Secretary to the second Lord Rothschild (the head of Britain's Zionist Federation) in 1917. It was a moment of particular Zionist fervour, and my grandfather shared in it, surprisingly in some ways. My mother was given to thinking of herself as insufficiently 'rapturous' in her commitment to Judaism, haunted by a sense of failing to live up to her mother's passionate involvement in Judaism, and especially in Hebrew scholarship. Nina had been very seriously encouraged in this by her own father, who had returned to the fold from a family which had long been assimilated to the point of repudiating their Jewish background. If it is possible to feel that rapture of any kind was not part of my grandfather's behavioural repertoire, a long letter he wrote to Chaim Weizmann in 1949, congratulating him on his book *Trial and Error* and on the success of Weizmann's efforts on behalf of Zionism, does at least express great enthusiasm for Israel, but also for 'our beloved England' and its part in it all. He wrote in his old age that for the first twenty-six years of his life he had been a Victorian English person who voted Conservative and later Liberal, but that he had found himself 'growing increasingly radical'. He had, he wrote, initially warmed to communism; and it is possible to feel surprised that he never mentions Marx in his book about the potato (though Engels appears in his bibliography), since the overall character of his analysis has clear Marxist affinities. He certainly voted for the Labour Party in at least the last two general elections of his life, encouraged by their development of the welfare state and particularly of the National Health Service. I remember that two cars set off from the house at one election: a Conservative one for most of the servants and a Labour one for my grandfather and one or two friends from the village.

There is no doubt, however, of his enthusiasm for the prospect of a Jewish homeland when he was a young man and of his continuing support for Israel as he grew older. He wrote later that Zionism had at first been no more for him than an understandable reaction 'induced in my fellow Jews of foreign origin by an unfriendly and alien environment'. The Balfour Declaration and his time in Palestine during the war changed that. A reading of *Palestine Reclaimed* makes it clear that this is the promised land for him too, as he writes to his wife, and that if they had been younger they might have chosen to live there. His excitement at the prospect of Jews settling and farming this land is palpable. His letters home are anyway strategically upbeat: he didn't want Nina to worry about him. But clearly he was enjoying this adventure: travelling, negotiating, lecturing the men in his battalion, meeting Jewish settlers, English colonists, some Arabs, even 'a highly cultured and refined anti-semite'. His most demanding task was the setting up of a makeshift hospital camp to treat two hundred soldiers during a serious malaria epidemic. He rode across the desert, marvelled at the scenery and the poverty, and wrote, 'I remain imperturbable and the work is not a bit beyond me.' He was contemptuous of some of those he met, however: especially the Yemenite Jews, 'poor stuff' on the whole, he thought, and even more so, 'the Arab', who 'has done so poorly and so little with the land that the Jew who means to work has an easy lead'. Nor was he, he assured Nina, a 'weak-kneed Jew' of the sort to be found among members of the League of British Jews at home, let alone a man like Edwin Montagu, who, as

Secretary of State for India at the time, was firmly warning the British government at that very moment against recognising Palestine as 'a national home' for the Jews.

These were early days, and as A. J. P. Taylor has put it, 'Palestine was at this time inhabited predominantly by Arabs, a fact which the British government brushed lightly aside.' Most Jews appear to have brushed it aside too, as my grandfather did. He was clear about the character of his Zionism, which was not like the Zionism of 'those of our men — and there are quite a few genuine souls — who love the land, the very soil, as such, because it is the land of their fathers. I do not feel this. I love the land because its inspiration is a necessary factor in Jewish evolution.' Zionism for him was, he wrote, 'much more scientific than idealistic'. This was a chance to effect a (relatively) benign eugenics experiment. No sterilisation, no manipulation of birth rates, no weeding out of the sub-standard, but a demonstration that the best Jewish 'types'(and he found plenty of examples of these already in Palestine), if given the opportunity to control their own destiny, would show superior adaptability, intelligence and determination, and create something of value to the world and themselves. He was always convinced that his own family, and indeed most Anglo-Jews, were neither as learned nor as enterprising as the Jews — not religious ones, for the most part — who were leaving Russia and Poland for Palestine. He had faith in what he perceived as the ardent determination of these Eastern Europeans to create a new life and even, in the language of eugenics, to breed new people, a new race, physically strong, practical and inventive, and aggressive in their own defence.

Appended to his *Palestine Reclaimed* is a bizarre lecture he delivered to his battalion in Cairo, in which he proposes a complex history of Jewish dispersal and intermarriage (or 'extra-marriage' as he later called what he saw as potentially 'the most destructive' force in contemporary Judaism) in order to distinguish different Jewish physical types, but also to explain the persistence of certain recognisably Jewish physiognomies and characteristics. It has been remarked before that most eugenics enthusiasts have started from the position that they themselves represented an especially desirable human norm. My grandfather was no exception. He dismisses Sephardi claims to some sort of Jewish aristocracy by reminding his audience that most Sephardim look as they do and are as they are because of intermarriage with Spaniards, Portuguese or North Africans. The book regrets racial impurity (while showing an incipiently experimental, and indeed Mendelian, interest in the products of mixed marriages – of which I was to be one, as it happens) and rehearses stereotypical views of Arabs as 'thieving'

and as devoid of any redeeming sense of solidarity, and
of so-called Oriental Jews as being more or less indis-
tinguishable from them. The British come well out of
it all, as do the Jews who are most like them. His interest
in racial categories and characteristics was to persist and
to involve him in collecting photographs for an album
of facial types and in acrimonious as well as friendlier
arguments. By no means all his correspondents agreed
with his theory of recessive Jewish genes, likely to lose
out in the offspring of a mixed marriage, or with his
rather crude distinguishing of 'Jewish looks' as rounded
rather than angular. Harold Laski was clearly infuriated
by a letter from Redcliffe on the subject in 1912 and
replied on a postcard:

> I thank you for your interesting if somewhat dog-
> matic letter. It seems to me that we differ funda-
> mentally in our conception not only of scientific
> method but also of what are to be called scientific
> facts, and agreement is hardly possible. I shall be
> very glad to avail myself sometime of your invita-
> tion to see your potatoes.

It is possible to regard Redcliffe's fascination with racial
categories and characteristics as in part a retaliatory move
against those who were beginning to use eugenics to
justify sterilisation, particularly of immigrants to America
and of Jews. In England, there had been work by Sidney
and Beatrice Webb and others which showed that Jews
as well as Catholics had a higher birth rate than the rest
of the population, and which argued that this could lead
to deterioration of the national stock.

Reclaiming Palestine is a difficult book to read at the

beginning of the twenty-first century, in the wake of a dubiously righteous war in Afghanistan and with the prospect of a cataclysmic conflagration in the Middle East. Nor is the current agonising impasse in Israel unimaginable as an outcome for any reader of my grandfather's lyrical account of this promising new world:

> They are very conscious that they are re-building, and they feel the responsibility. They realise that their method is tentative, but they equally are determined to have a world to live in that shall not be cursed from the beginning by the old ideas of property and feudalism . . .
>
> I believe in Jews. They are wonderful. We have the highest and the lowest . . . They are difficult, and try every nerve in your body – but where are there such idealists and where a people that, after the cruellest degradation, can spring forth and blossom anew in a single generation?

The difficulty is not just with the eugenics undercurrent and its occasional lurid surfacing, nor with the easy assignment of racial superiority and inferiority, but with the justification this allows for contempt for the poor and historically oppressed inhabitants of Palestine and for what is seen as their lack of unity and national pride. Benny Morris writes in his book *Righteous Victims: A History of the Zionist–Arab Conflict, 1881–2001* that 'Zionism emerged about a quarter of a century earlier than Arab nationalism, a head start in political consciousness and organization that proved vital to the Jews' success and to the Palestinian Arabs' failure during the following decades of conflict.' By the time Redcliffe started to consider the causes of Irish famine and death from starvation and emigration in the middle of the nineteenth century, he had developed an intricate historical understanding and analysis. Here he is still seeking racial explanations for Arab 'failure' in Palestine, ignoring both recent and older history in his criticism of the Arab population of Palestine and appearing to be satisfied with simplicities. When the book was later reprinted in serial form in a British Zionist publication, he insisted that all hostile remarks about Arabs be omitted from it.

Daniel Kevles points out in his *In the Name of Eugenics* that this movement – whether in its more statistical strain as developed by Galton and his followers at University College London, or in its genetic and experimental forms, fostered to some extent by a return to the ideas of Mendel – gathered some high-minded apostles, and that 'enthusiasm was highest among social radicals'. My grandfather, who had as a young man distrusted 'the Arab' as the representative of a heterogeneous, and therefore weakened, race, was later to oppose exactly that kind of racial typecasting as explanation. He learned from what happened to the Jews in Hitler's Europe in the 1940s; but almost his only references to that in his 1949 book on the potato are made in the context of reminding his readers that 'the picture of Hitler's Europe is probably no more tragic than was that of Ireland in 1603' and of arguing against those who blamed the Irish character or inheritance for Irish misfortunes:

> It was not till Gladstone attacked the Irish problem, that English legislators began to realise that the degradation of the people was due primarily to an inequitable land system allied to an aggressive

Protestant policy of Ascendancy. Nor is it yet realised
that the universal dependence of the people on the
potato was the economic consequence of such a
policy. It was a dependence which inevitably reduced
the social standards of the people to one commensurate with the cheapness of its culture, the abun-
dance of its crop, and the ease of its storage.

The runaway success of the eugenics movement at the
beginning of the twentieth century, born from an alliance
of social statistics and genetics, and devoted in its own
eyes to the improvement of human societies, could be
said to have been hobbled and eventually brought down
by its neglect of history as well as its abandonment of
common sense. Just before he left Palestine in 1919,
Redcliffe wrote to Nina: 'The Arab question is not so
difficult as people think. Just now our opponents naturally make the most of it, but there is room for both.'
The problems, he believed, were economic and not political, matters of land and labour rather than power and
control. In his later work, where he is considering the
vital importance (and the hazards) for past societies of
producing cheap food, he would not so cavalierly iso-
late the economic from the political and the historical.
Perhaps, though, that transformation was already beginning for him in Palestine, for he was sorry to learn in
1919 that their old friend Israel Zangwill was campaigning to clear 'the Arab out bag and baggage': that
would be 'simply ridiculous and only comparable to
Cromwell's effort in Ireland'. Nina hastened to assure
him that 'Israel says everyone has misunderstood what
he has said about the Arabs. He never meant to drive
them out, but to come to an amicable arrangement with

them.' Redcliffe registered this as a long footnote in his book: too long to be entirely convincing. He hoped that their other old friend, Herbert Samuel, would be offered and would accept the difficult post of Governor, as indeed he did in the following year. Nina reported an early morning visit from Samuel, just before he left for Palestine. He wanted reassurance, it seems, and he wanted his friends to visit him and even to consider moving to Palestine for good.

Writing about a third old friend, the classicist Francis Cornford, Redcliffe contrasts his friend's interest in philosophy with his own desire to 'invent' philosophies and theories. This is offered in part as a contrast between a philosopher and scholar, on the one hand, and a scientist given to hypotheses, on the other. But Redcliffe's theorising went further than that. He spent a good deal of his life trying to settle to his own satisfaction the nature of Jewishness, rearranging what he saw as its constituent parts: race, nation, religion. Some notion of 'race' seemed to him essential, though he worried at definitions and confusions and impurities. Later, he wrote that 'the Jews are not a Race, they are an inbreeding Family in which certain types tend, so to speak, to crystallize out'. 'Nation' might one day mean Israel, but in practice experience of 'nation' differed so radically for Jews in Britain from that of those forced out of or still suffering in Eastern Europe as to come to seem empty of meaning. So what was left if you subtracted religion, ritual, authoritative texts and voices, as he felt increasingly inclined to?

He thought of himself as deaf to mysticism but responsive to nature. Reproved as a 'romantic' by his more adamantly sceptical friend Charles Singer, a medical and scientific historian who, in a letter to Redcliffe, referred to most Orthodox Jewish practice (*kashrut*), as 'a mass of highly sophisticated bosh, based on practices of a low anthropologic order', and to *shehitah* (traditional Jewish methods of slaughtering animals) 'as one of those odd survivals of savagery, like fox hunting, or caste, or suttee', my grandfather was obliged to admit his own ambivalence in these matters:

> It is possible to present orthodoxy in a very beautiful garb, and to deck it out, as did my Nina and Herbert Loewe, in a shining garment of poetic symbolism . . . to the majority and to all who do not know of or cannot appreciate this poetic interpretation, it is deadening and, because it usurps the place of true ethics, positively dangerous.

Nina may have been responsible for some of her husband's ambivalence and his romanticism. She first caught his eye in the gallery of the New West End Synagogue in London, one of several synagogues he went to irregularly as a young man. 'There I saw a young woman directly opposite who stood out from all others by reason of her stately figure and her truly queenly beauty,' he wrote. They were engaged ten days later and married within four months. They appear to have been very happy together, and he remained awestruck by her beauty and brilliance. Their five surviving children continued through long lives to remember the beauty and the brilliance, but to wonder whether she hadn't also been singularly lacking in humour and warmth. She decided very early, apparently, that her oldest son should become a rabbi and must have felt some disappointment when

he changed from classical and Hebrew studies to Natural Sciences on his arrival in Cambridge. Her sometimes glum replies to Redcliffe's letters during the First World War arc understandable. She must have missed him, had a lot on her plate looking after a large household without him in wartime and, perhaps most of all, wished that she could be in Palestine too. It was she who wrote the 'Marching Song' for her husband's Judean Battalion (set to music by her children's piano teacher), and she who was at that very moment collecting inspiring Zionist poems and songs and stories for an anthology for Jewish children called *Apples and Honey*, and publishing slim volumes of poetry infused with a somewhat indeterminate love for God and man.

And then, in late 1919, when Redcliffe finally came home from the war, she was diagnosed with bowel cancer. For the next five years she gradually became more ill, mostly at home, carried about on a contraption Redcliffe built for her and visited by her learned Jewish friends and by Frances Cornford, the poet and wife of the philosopher, who came to see her from Cambridge at least once a week. The painter William Rothenstein, who visited her during her illness, wrote of her resemblance then and always to 'the virtuous woman of the Old Testament'. She died at home in 1925 at forty-eight, and it is possible that those last years completed some sort of family embalming or canonisation. Her daughters were kept in the dark about the seriousness of their mother's illness and were utterly taken aback by her death, which they were then discouraged from mentioning. Both were instantly sent away, the fifteen-year-old, my mother, back to boarding school (a letter she wrote home only two weeks later is full of cheering jokes and drawings for her father and does not mention her dead mother), the ten-year-old to stay with a somewhat grimly Orthodox family in Oxford. She never forgot the horror of that exile. My grandfather found his new solitude unbearable, and besides requiring his sons to keep him constant company, appears to have been determined to find a new wife as soon as possible.

Memories of my grandfather began to slip and slide as soon as I let in the contents of those brown boxes in the Cambridge University Library. Whether comfortably or not – and how should I know? – it turns out that

Redcliffe always lived, if gracefully, with multiplicity and ambivalence. His first wife was probably central to this. His love and loyalty and his pride in her had to coexist with being a scientist, an agnostic Jew, a responsible and patriotic Englishman, and then, for the second half of his life, with her death and his remarriage. He reacted instinctively against extremes and mystifications, but his love and respect for Nina entailed the suppression of much of his natural scepticism, whether about Orthodox Judaism or racial character. She also represented a world of poetry and the spirit, the beautiful mysteries of medieval Hebrew literature, and he was loath, even long after her death, to do without some contact with those things; though, as he wrote, 'the data which we estab-lish by means of our reason and intellect are . . . immune to attack from the dogmatic pronouncements of the reli-gious'. It wasn't until he began to suspend his theorising, whether about race or Jewishness or Israel or even the genetics of the potato, and to put it to the service of history and historical thinking, that his real talents and passions were revealed.

The Lucien Wolf Memorial Lecture, delivered by Redcliffe in London in 1953, when he was seventy-eight, was probably intended as some sort of resolution of his old ambivalence, and it was characteristically public. It was a lament for the old 'Anglo-Jewry, in spirit somno-lent and in practice latitudinarian', or, as Todd Endelman has put it, 'the decline of moderate traditionalism in Anglo-Jewish practice' and 'the ascendance of right-wing views and standards'. It was also a warning against what Redcliffe saw as a new and 'highly developed legalism' that was gaining ground among British Jews. This new orthodoxy and authoritarianism would put off the young, he believed, and that would be a disaster. He remembered a time when

> in the community at large there was, if not religious peace, at least an atmosphere of kindly make-believe and gentlemanly behaviour which for long had been no inadequate substitute. That it covered much indifference and more ignorance, distressed neither leaders nor led. A sense of brotherhood and the acceptance of collective responsibility was then, as now, a firmer bond than religion in our time is ever likely to be.

And he made no bones about the continuing duties of the Anglo-Jewish community, as he saw them:

> Before the outbreak of the first war, the community was so well integrated, so conscious of its three-fold task, the maintenance of its poor, the avoidance of any occasion for ill feeling at home, and the assistance and protection of its brethren abroad, that neither religious nor lay leaders were unduly concerned with the attitude of the individual towards religious observance or belief.

Several pillars of the community walked out of the lecture, and the Chief Rabbi interrupted to describe it as a 'castigation of Orthodoxy, one which is painful to those of us who hold dear everything Jewish'. My grandfather replied firmly that 'I must speak the truth as I find it', and continued to list those practices he most abhorred: preventing the children of mixed marriages from attending classes in a synagogue, for instance (something he fought for on behalf of one of my sisters), most dietary laws and the Jewish method of slaughtering animals, which could no longer be defended on humanitarian or scientific grounds since the introduction of electrical stunning. It was this last issue more than any other that incensed his audience, though Endelman suggests that much of their bitterness derived from 'resentment of the old communal élite, the network of long-anglicized, well-to-do families who governed Anglo-Jewry before World War II'. The acrimony lingered long after the lecture, and there were fierce objections to its being published. When it was, eventually, it was with emendations that Redcliffe had accepted with reluctance.

This was a painful episode, which may have hastened his death. Yet it seemed to me then (as it does now) a brave performance, which he had a right to feel proud of, as I think he did, though the public and exposing character of the quarrel offended him. Apart from the difficult questions it raised about loyalty and versions of what Judaism is and should be, his argument maddened many Jews by invoking science and modernity, by relying on an expectation of reciprocity between majority and minority groups in contemporary Britain, and by asking what the roles of tradition and ritual should be and whether they were sufficiently open to change, modernisation. It made him enemies, and a good deal of the Jewish press was savagely antagonistic. An old friend from a similar background suggested that Redcliffe was now 'in the same camp as the anti-semitic gutter press'. It is likely that he was in fact moved far more by the need to reduce provocations to anti-semitism than by any especially tender feelings for animals.

Perhaps all brown boxes in hot and hermetically sealed

manuscript rooms have the potential to disturb memories of paradise and its Olympian inhabitants. I think we all knew as children that this was a way of life that was rare and disappearing. My mother taught us to think of ourselves as belonging to a different class from her father and stepmother. Our parents lived in smallish town houses, with 'help' of various kinds, but no 'servants'. And our fathers and some of our mothers went off to work and earned their livings. Our fathers were not patriarchs nor our mothers goddesses. Every ten years or so Redcliffe revised the letter he hoped his children would eventually read after his death. It made recommendations about furniture, pictures, books to be kept in the family, while others might be given to museums or libraries. He asked to be buried next to Nina (in an Orthodox Jewish graveyard in North London), adding that 'it may be sentimental but I really think it would be truer to regard it as "patriarchal"'. He would not have been surprised to learn that by the end of the twentieth century the family had been told firmly that they had no business holding on to burial sites they had owned for a hundred years or more, given their record as agnostics and atheists. Perhaps, on second thoughts, he would have been a little surprised by the robustness of that rejection and by the schisms and orthodoxies and fundamentalism which it announced and which could be said to define a good deal of what has so far characterised this new century.

Three Sisters

I sometimes think my sisters don't believe a word I say, that they came into the world armed with the most vigilant scepticism as to their older sister's capacity to tell the truth. This has been a useful strategy, whether innate or acquired – with its 'but surely's' and 'Oh, I don't think so's' – particularly for pursuing their lifelong ambition of penetrating the oppressive cloud that may be cast, I am told, by an older sibling, while also avoiding all contamination by role model. I don't always bother to remonstrate with them, and, of course, I have a different story to tell.

Occasionally I have intimations of bliss, of a time before I had sisters, when I was, or anyway might have been, the apple of my parents' eye. I have no clear memories of this, I should say; but stories, pictures, photographs encourage me to dream. I have inherited a small drawing by my mother which she sent as a present to her oldest brother from Paris, where my parents lived for the first three years of their married life. Against elegant grey shutters, my parents sleep, post-coitally close on their narrow bed, as I do not remember them, while their baby daughter sits up, back straight in her wooden cot, patiently waiting for these sleepers to open their eyes and contemplate her with their usual unadulterated delight. I am momentarily transported to an Eden of smiling approval. I have been told stories of my lisping

French during holidays in England, of a cat formally named 'Chat' by my grandparents in the wake of one visit. I certainly gazed into the camera confidently enough, though I dare say that's not much to go on.

The fall from heaven, just before my third birthday, is accompanied by more substantial memories: a rough Channel crossing, rain in a London street, a tall three-sided strawberry water ice bought from an ice-cream man on a bicycle, a new red oilskin mackintosh and sou'wester, and excited anticipation as my father took me to see my mysteriously missing mother in a room filled by her bed and a crib. Well, that was that, I suppose, though I seem to have tried to delay recognition of how things were to be from now on until the last possible moment. I refused to look in that crib then or later, though I was said to have rocked the pram after the baby was brought home so violently that it almost fell off the flat bit of our roof in Highgate, in North London, where it had been placed by the irresponsible nanny I understood to have been sent in the post by my grandfather to save the day.

Juliet Mitchell's *Mad Men and Medusas* is a marvellously garrulous story of the ups and downs, as it were, met with by hysteria as a descriptive diagnosis within anthropological and psychoanalytic studies. In retrieving hysteria from its protean and intermittent history, and

particularly from its entanglements with accounts of femininity, she attributes its persistence as a phenomenon – as well as denials of its persistence – to siblings and to their somewhat unreliable presence within developmental and psychoanalytic theory. 'The sibling relationship is important,' she tells us, 'because, unlike the parental relationship, it is our first *social* relationship.' Whether that is fair or not to parental relations, which become 'social' pretty quickly, after all, it seems useful to think of sibling relations as models for a range of 'lateral' ones: with friends, rivals, lovers, spouses, fellow workers, and so on. To some extent Mitchell is reversing traditional Freudian priorities when she writes that 'feelings for siblings and peers cast their shadow over relations with parents'.

Mitchell may sometimes struggle in her efforts to yoke hysteria to sibling relations, but investigating them in tandem and through example opens up abundant possibilities. Part of her purpose is certainly to reclaim hysteria, but as a universal phenomenon, which is always 'the deployment of weakness as power', whatever its local manifestations, though these all tend to rely on illness of some kind to gain or hold the attention of others. As a form of protest likely to be made by those who experience themselves as inferior, hysteria is also likely to be associated with women, less in any biological sense than in terms of Freud's assertion of a universal tendency for both sexes to repudiate femininity. But since it is important for Mitchell to insist on the presence of male hysteria she uses Mozart's Don Giovanni and Shakespeare's Iago to do so, arguing that suppressed jealousy in both characters drives them to compulsive behaviour that can be counted on to produce that emotion in other people.

The new baby remained a baby as far as I was concerned, and beneath my notice. I went off each morning
to a kindergarten round the corner (I like to think it
was the one where Elizabeth Taylor was sent at about
that time), and the photographer came on the day I wet
my knickers, an event recorded for posterity as I sat
uncomfortably dressed in someone else's spare ones. We
are all sitting on a bench in a small dank London back
garden, made especially sunless by the overhanging
chestnut tree, though several of us wear our obligatory
sunhats with elastic under the chin. There is no sign of
Elizabeth Taylor. I wore a green linen tunic with a girdle
for the eurhythmics class I went to at Byron House,
another school further up the hill, and I envied my
slightly older cousins for many things, but especially
because they were at school there all day and due to
proceed to the Channing School for Girls at the top of
the hill before long. I had my tonsils and adenoids taken
out at about that time in the Great Ormond Street
Children's Hospital, where I received further confirmation of my fall from grace when my mother gave presents
to all the other children in the ward which were in no
way inferior to the one she gave me. My little sister
comes out of her pram from time to time, but my
memory keeps her safely out of sight until – appropriately enough – the coronation of King George VI in
1937, when she and I wore identical shepherdess dresses
and danced at the party held in the village hall where
my grandparents lived. That may have been the first time
I realised that grown-ups warmed to the sight of two
little girls who looked and were dressed alike, but also
that the smaller and younger you were the better.

The sense I have of my charms being effortlessly

eclipsed by those of my sister colours memories of other visits to the Hertfordshire village where my maternal and Jewish grandparents lived and where we mingled at holiday time with cousins and uncles and aunts, and all the children ate en masse in the servants' hall. I know I worked hard and perhaps desperately there and else-where to regain the limelight – showing off, it was called – and just as hard on the occasional visits to my father's ancient aunts and uncle (non-Jewish, as I learned to think of them) in their tall Hampstead house. I remember the kitchen and the white enamel contraption on the wall, on which words like 'sago' and 'currants' and 'tea' were written in dark blue letters, with little sliding doors to reveal a 'yes' by each word, to remind you to buy some more of them: a shopping list with pedagogic pur-poses, as it seemed to me even then, in a household where you were rated for your brains and not your charm.

The thirties are always prelapsarian, pre-sisters, pre-war and, as it happens, pre-illness for me, though I was just seven when they ended and by then the war had started and my illness was over. A clear memory from before my illness is of a book my father used to read to me called *Off the Chain*, about a boy losing his dog. My father thought the book ludicrous and read it in tones of fastidious derision, while I secretly thought it tragic beyond words, and could not have enough of it. I soon learned to disguise my true feelings with a superior smile, however, so that in later years the least allusion to that book or others like it has reminded me uncomfortably of my dissembling childhood self. Most of my memories of those years rely fitfully on lighting and come to mind as miniature theatrical tableaux, curiously immobilised and transfixed. I remember houses, rows of them, and shining wet pavements, no doubt Paris ones as well as London ones. The streets are real, but peopled now by characters from photographs and films rather than memory.

I am interested in what Mitchell writes about siblings and especially about sisters. In recognising myself in her analysis, I am also hoping to find my younger sisters and their predicament, for what is shared by siblings all too easily blinds us to the differences: we are, after all, so many seedling lettuces planted out to ripen serially in our own time and climate. Ronald Fraser ends *In Search of a Past*, a historical and psychoanalytic excavation of the gentry world he inhabited as a child born in 1930, with a conversation he had as an adult with a brother six years younger than himself. They discover that their memories of their mother might be of two different people: that she was a creature of history, as they were, and transformed by the years of the Second World War from a shy, distant grande dame to a practical woman, who looked after the younger son herself and, because of rationing and the development of an elaborate local black market, made alliances with people in the village. These changes later seemed to both her sons to have heralded a welcome and absolute break with debilitating class expectations.

Mitchell's 'catastrophe' of sibling displacement may indeed be the first discovery that we are replaceable and not unique, but the frowning cast and chorus attendant on that catastrophe may grow older, wiser, sadder, or, I suppose, sillier: the world and its inhabitants as well as the family drama itself will have changed, moved on. The advent of a new sibling may well be experienced as a version of Lacan's 'mirror image' and of the simultaneous learning of 'I' as exclusively ours as well as not ours; except that those transformative moments happen, not in theory, but in real time.

Less than two years separated my sister's birth from my being diagnosed as having a tubercular gland. Dr Leo Rau was our doctor then, his name always pronounced with the rasping gurgle he went in for when recommending raspberries or himself. He lived with his family in the only perfectly minimalist flat I have ever been in, palely covering an entire floor of High Point, a marvel of modern architecture, only completed in 1935. It must have been talked about at the time, since I seem always to have known it was connected (and confused for me) with that other Berthold Lubetkin creation of the 1930s, the Penguin Pool at London Zoo. Dr Rau, a robust and noisy refugee from Germany, prescribed X-rays for me in a machine like a gigantic steel waffle-maker as well as raspberries, boiled milk and bed. He seems also to have been the one to propose exile to Broadstairs by the sea in Kent and to have discovered the nursing home where I spent the next nine months.

Sending young children away from home was more common in the thirties than it is now. I have a friend who was sent away from home with a doctor's approval before he had even got to his first birthday, and for quite a long time, because an autocratic grandmother thought him 'too close' to his mother. I knew children younger than five who were sent to boarding school. Considered from here, more than sixty years later, my parents' readiness to do Dr Rau's bidding and send me away seems excessive, unnecessary, hard to explain. I don't remember feeling ill, though I think I coughed a bit, and there may have been a fear that my sister would catch whatever I had. Perhaps more worldly members of both my parents' families put pressure on them. My grandfather had had TB as a young man and recovered from it after two years or so spent in Switzerland, and there had been talk of my going there too. Fear of an imminent war saved me from that. I think the whole episode embarrassed my parents and made them ashamed. TB was becoming an illness associated with poverty and dirt and carelessness as well as unpasteurised milk, and there were still no drugs to cure it. Years later I applied to the American Embassy for an immigrant visa, so that I might get paid work in Harvard, where my future husband had gone on a fellowship. Dr Rau was thinner and less ebullient by now as he examined my X-rays. There was no scar to be seen, he assured me, and no reason to confess to having had TB at all as I swore to leave the American constitution as I found it. I should have asked him then why it had been thought necessary to send me away from home in that case. I did not press my sister on the point either, when, as someone who has been a doctor all her adult life, she told me not long ago that I had probably never had TB at all.

Who knows? A hysterical illness perhaps, and a self-procured exile? I was happy in Broadstairs, on holiday in this holiday resort: the youngest of the eight children who were there to convalesce and probably the least ill. It is true that I felt humiliated to be seen at the age of five in a large wickerwork baby carriage on the beach – a punishment for something or other, as I saw it – but that wasn't for long. My parents visited me once or twice and left me with presents: seven handkerchiefs, I remember, for each day of the week and for each of Snow White's dwarves, which I soaked with dutiful tears when they left and spread sensibly to dry across the hot pipe by my bed. I learned to read and write there and took momentarily to praying on my knees and to Sunday churchgoing, activities I associated unequivocally with sin and my own bad character. I remember wearing my pink coat with its maroon velvet collar and walking carefully down a path edged with stinging nettles from the back garden to the church, my feet protected by white socks and Start-Rite shoes. There were funerals while I was there: for the oldest of the patients, a boy of twenty, and for one of the two sisters who ran the home. I think those occasions put me off God for life. But I wasn't sad there, or rather I was much sadder for my parents than for myself, for I liked to imagine them bereft without me. I think now that my exile by the sea confirmed an instinctive sense of myself as an only child and made me long – more than anything – to be able to swim. Away from my sister and my guilty, worried, incompetent parents, I could imagine myself for a little longer as I wanted to be: unique, possibly an orphan and wholly irreplaceable. We have heard about the only child's dream of siblings. There is also the sibling's dream of being an only child.

Coming home meant re-entry into something I barely recognised and probably never learned to. It was the summer just before 'Munich', and my parents had moved from Highgate to Petersfield in Hampshire while I was away. My father was certain there would be another war and had taken a job teaching the piano at Bedales, the school where he and my mother had been as children. They had bought for £1,000, and with their usual disregard for charm or convenience, a house by the railway station, which shuddered as the level-crossing gates swung into position for the trains to pass. Its discomforts persuaded my grandfather to stay in a local hotel on his one visit to his daughter. Strangely, this new house was as full of illness and contagion as the old one had been. My sister was getting over whooping cough, and I was to be kept away from her for another two weeks. I remember with clarity and a sinking heart the vision of my small and carelessly forgotten sister, alert, shy, wary against the light from the room behind her, as she sat by the dark-haired nanny of the day, at the other end of the long passage leading from my father's music room to the nursery. I must have known then that she had always been there, that my parents were not and had never been bereft and that I was not cut out for this new life as a sister.

I was nearly nine and by now a big, bad sister even in my own eyes when my second sister was born in 1941 and all the most dramatic changes brought about by the war were already in place and for eternity, as it seemed. I looked forward to this birth and this child, whom I believed would be mine in some way, though I was teased about my mother's pregnancy at school and must have felt some forebodings. I had taken the precaution of warning my existing sister that she would probably be given away once the new baby was born, since she was adopted anyway and likely, as I expressed it to her, to be found redundant. Perhaps her scepticism began there and then. She wisely refused to believe me. I also managed to burn down the top floor of the house at that time, but I have written about that before. My mother was to become confident and relaxed with this new child, whom she brought up without help, something she had not done since the years in Paris with me. It never seemed surprising that she should get on best with this late, wartime child and love her most easily.

This was not a 'catastrophe' for me as the earlier birth had been, though I expect it confirmed my three-year-old's belief that my parents would only have bothered to have another child if the one they had was in some way inadequate to requirements; and I have always felt my substitutability as a judgement of some kind. I certainly came to feel responsible for all this boylessness, so stoically borne – or so I believed – by my parents. My father made rather a show of being relieved: a boy would have been dreadfully spoiled, he'd say airily, without specifying who would do the spoiling or why. We were now three sisters, and my father's allusions to King Lear's daughters, to Cinderella and her sisters, to the witches in *Macbeth*, were, as was usual with him, jocular and unanswerable. Sometimes he would add wryly that if he'd had his way he would have called us Marjory, Perjury and Forgery: in that order, for which I was quietly grateful. We became a family weighted numerically and somehow comically towards the female; though in fantasy, it seems to me, we were singly and collectively drawn to everything male. My mother's smuggling into the house magazines like *Woman* or *Woman's Own* if one of us was ill in bed only strengthened this bias.

Freud wrote that he had never known a woman who did not dream of murdering her siblings; and though Juliet Mitchell goes on to argue that such murderousness is by no means confined to women, she also concedes that 'the dethronement will be different for girls and boys' since 'the girl may be more often or more seriously displaced within the patrilineage than the boy' and anyway there are weaker taboos against murdering one's sister than murdering one's brother. Besides, if hysteria is provoked by a longing for what one has not got, it could well be that such longing really is more capacious for girls. My father decided early on that sisterly quarrels were trivial matters, best dealt with through ridicule and assurances that we all loved each other really; and my mother sometimes took the view that discussion of sisters and what you feel about them is simply a forbidden topic. I suspect that she knew something at first hand about hysterical, murderous desires and useless struggles for a share of the slim pickings available to a fifth child who is a girl – and the only one for five years, in her case – who is then presented with the troubling gift of a delightful little sister.

For Mitchell, the question a child asks is not about

who they are, about identity, but 'What is my position in this kinship scenario?' and the question is bound to be inflected by gender and place in the family.

A younger sibling is a repetition of the older child, occupying the place it previously had; an older sibling monopolizes the place the subject thought it shared. The response is like the territoriality of many animals transposed into the context of human kinship — if one's space is invaded, this is experienced as what indeed in a sense it actually *is*: a catastrophe.

It has not always been easy to recognise the calamity I have been for my sisters: Mitchell's analysis may help. Much has been expected of sisterhood, and it has

meant many things. Feminism has sometimes relied on sisterliness for a politics grounded riskily in nature rather than in the infinite variety of accommodations that are made to nature, and we have all felt rebuked by suggestions that what we said or felt or did about other women was somehow 'not very sisterly'. Brotherly love is also assumed to be an unquestionable good in its metaphorical passage from siblings to the wider world, and it may be that jealousy and rivalry between brothers is tolerated more readily than such feelings between girls, just as other forms of competition are. The love – natural, inexhaustible, unruffled – which has been presumed to exist (surely unwarrantably) between the Austen sisters or among the Brontës, say, has been allowed to stand in for more diffuse expectations of the sympathy that must inevitably follow from what women share naturally and as a consequence of their dependent or even parasitical social experience. Women are thought to respond to what is alike about them, or that is the hope. Even when men are said, puzzlingly, 'to love women' (on the model of loving dogs or horses, I take it) there is also a presumption that it is something we share and have in common that they love, though there are allowed to be some pretty stark contrasts and opposites contained within these similarities. Indeed, the good and the bad sister are familiar tropes: a play on likeness as somehow meant to trick us into ignoring what are then deemed to be barely visible but sinister differences between sisters.

And it is true that this supposed similarity can effectively mask or muddle the minute distinctions (often in areas which are especially important to us) which girls grow up perceiving among themselves. Sisters may represent our first go at this and our first benchmarks. No limb or other body part remained unmeasured, uncompared between me and the older of my two sisters. How readily sisters assign themselves (and are assigned) roles: 'the clever one' or 'the thin one' or 'the beauty'. 'She's artistic or athletic or . . .' on and on, even among gaggles of girls, where beauty, brains, talent may be pretty evenly allotted or perhaps – 'surely not?' – in quite short supply. It is as if the two/three/four girls in a family have to carve out their share of the rather sparse array of virtues and talents available to them. One of my sisters danced and subsequently went to ballet school, for which I envied her excessively and unavailingly, though she became a doctor in the end. The other sister distinguished herself by doing well at maths and science but too late really for my envy or useless emulation to kick in. But our apparent similarity hid then, as it hides now, more than our differences. It has sometimes served to deny the reality and the truth of our separate visions and versions of the past, as well as of what really was shared (if uncomfortably) in our childhood and inheritance. The world around us changed, just as we did. No wonder my sisters find it hard to believe what I tell them.

I used to think the war would never end. Everything 'pre-war' was simultaneously recalled as better, rarer, finer, more sumptuous, while also coming to stand for a general miasma of shabbiness, the past, a world full of everything that was out of date and beneath contempt. 'Lashings' of cream and butter, pyramids of eggs and string-bags full of oranges and bananas took time to fade as gleaming images of luxury and excess from 'before the war'. Buildings, even those untouched by bombing, fell into serious disrepair, and I remember my astonished pleasure after the war at the sight of painted window frames and front doors and replaced railings. My parents longed for France, for travel abroad, for their Paris friends. They heard nothing after 1940. My father listened perpetually to the wireless and read books by famous major generals. He worried about the news, the blackout, possible invasion – for on a properly blacked-out night we could be said to be vulnerable if you drew a straight line from Portsmouth through Aldershot to London. I believed the story that we would be saved by the brilliantly dreamed-up ruse of altering the road signs, so that intrepid Germans making their way northwards to London would find themselves permanently mired in Winchester or heading for Cornwall. We were each fitted with gas masks in lovely little boxes you wore slung across your chest. My sister's had a Mickey Mouse face to tempt her into it.

My father joined the Home Guard in 1940, and before long he was put in possession of one of the platoon's few guns, which he kept behind his armchair in our sitting room and never fired, as far as I know. On the one occasion I actually saw him with it he fainted on parade, perhaps from the heat of a wartime summer's day and his scratchy, khaki uniform. Three handsome working-class boys from South London were sent to us as evacuees in order to pursue their grammar school education away from the bombs. One of them taught me to climb drainpipes and died of alcoholism ten years or so after getting a first in French at Oxford just after the war. Another was killed at the front less than two years after he left us, before he was twenty. There were visits from refugees brought out of Germany or Austria by my grandfather. I remember one elderly widow of cornucopian culture, possessing nothing, it seemed, but a small portfolio of her dead husband's exquisite woodcuts, who deplored my philistine ways and blamed my often frantic mother for them. She must have stayed for several months. We had lodgers and other guests, and visits from school or college friends of my mother's, who had become land girls or Wrens. My mother sometimes wept with exhaustion and exasperation as she felt for her Woodbines on the ledge above the stove, but she was learning to manage a complicated household, and I remember her as undeniably grown-up. By the time my youngest sister was born in 1941 my mother's long fair hair was practically white.

One or two bombs dropped nearby, it was thought by accident, though the Itshide rubber factory in the town was engaged in war work and may have been the lure. We knew we were lucky and that things were much worse in London. Rationing, coupons – for everything from sweets and tins of peaches to shoes and petrol – were what I remember best, and that some women in the family were thought to have found their métier as purveyors of tiny individual portions of butter or as dealers trading in the exchange of eggs for clothing coupons. 'Digging for Victory' posters were taken literally. My grandfather, that scientist and historian of the potato, put his large garden to the cultivation of his favourite vegetable, and wherever you went there were patches of onions and leeks in people's allotments and back gardens. You could eat, in what were called British Restaurants, 'agricultural' pies for 3d each with 'bubble and squeak' (a delicious fry-up of cabbage and mashed potatoes) on the side. I remember a visit to our local one in its huge Nissen hut when my second sister was still a baby in her pram.

People put Anderson air-raid shelters at the bottom of their gardens. They were hardly ever used, but were good for playing in, while other people did as we did: reinforced their cellars with iron girders and – imagining that we might survive a direct hit down there – usually left a few rusty, unappetising tins of spam and baked beans on a shelf, to assuage peckishness under bombardment. It is clear now that the extraordinary energy and ingenuity that went into this shift to wartime mode was often in excess of what was needed, but that it represented an intensity and excitement felt by people responding in whatever way they could to the imperatives of 'the war effort'. I have the sense that it channelled my parents' worry about themselves and their ability to bring up their children and in some ways lessened their anxiety. It may even have been that their difficult marriage became more manageable in the midst of the demands made on them by the war. On 8 May 1945, VE Day, I danced with my father in the town hall, an event so bizarrely uncharacteristic of him that it has remained a vivid and even triumphant memory ever since, publicly signalling my status as his first-born.

My mother died recently, and my sisters and I – grizzled orphan grandmothers – sift through the debris of our parents' lives, alighting occasionally on some surprising treasure, often unnoticed as well as uncherished in this house so seldom touched, adorned or added to. The altogether more glamorous relics of my parents' dead relations stand out strangely among the whitewood cupboards and bookcases and desks bought in their student days. The old scepticism among us has flourished with the invention of the email. We scrutinise, in provisional, uneasy alliance, photographs read for absences as much as presences, and identify, where we can, 'Sheraton' tables and 'celadon' pots and 'majolica' drug jars. Letters and diaries, temporarily put to one side to allay the anxiety they instantly awaken, are read later, in solitude. Lists are drawn up and distinctions made between 'the most uncomfortable armchair in the world' and the one which contrived to strike the back of your head even as you were collapsing into its broken springs. There is a shared refusal to allow the speech of any single one of us to proceed unaccompanied beyond the noun clause and into the thickets of the modal verb.

It's a Girl!

I'm still surprised to meet or read of women who recall the first signs of their adult femininity with pleasure. Here, for instance, is Julia Strachey – a writer capable of humour and irony on most aspects of her life – remembering the arrival of 'breasts and hips and so forth' as 'like a door opening on to my real self, on to a natural growth of generous giving, of loving, and everything that had been banned for me when I was still undeveloped – an extension of soul and accompanying body'. But then I was also a little taken aback when my daughter announced many years ago – she was four at the time – that she would certainly become a boy eventually, it was just a matter of waiting. Meanwhile, however, she planned to cut off her brother's 'willy' and attach it to herself with Sellotape to expedite the transformation. My interest in being or becoming a boy had been less graphically expressed (or imagined) than hers. I had no brother, and my intentions were more a matter of dress and general demeanour than of radical surgery. I thought of myself as a tomboy.

At the school I went to, Bedales – which still regarded itself as 'progressive' for teaching boys and girls together, and which had probably not changed much since my father, my mother and her brothers were there, or, indeed, since Julia Strachey had been there, only a little earlier (and very funny she is about Bedales and its absurder optimisms) – I learned that boys were simply and obviously better than girls. They wore serious grey flannel shorts and shirts, for a start, and were possessors of knowledge with a known market value: the Football League winners from as far back as 1902, for instance, and every one of Mozart's Köchel numbers. Boys also had rotten handwriting, read aloud stumblingly, were often unable to tie their own shoelaces and were rude to teachers. They were also quite often smelly and dirty. These were

failings, it seemed to me, which may be safely indulged by those who are sure of their superiority. In addition, the best of them ran faster than us, became expert traders and gamblers at an early age, were smaller and braver and seemed to care so much less than we did about their reputations. These were admirable qualities, and I wished they were mine. I wanted my hair cut like theirs and shorts without pleats – privileges which were firmly denied me. By then I could swim and dive better than the boys could and even run as fast and climb as high as most of them, though I experienced nearly over-whelming fear as I did some of these things. I once knocked down a large bully (I think inadvertently) and made his nose bleed, and I may have expected this ter-rifying act to clinch my membership of what I thought of as the boys' gang. For I believed that what boys wanted of a girl was that she reveal herself to be a 'good sort' and not different from them in essentials.

I remember these things ruefully, perplexed by what were in fact the beginnings of a blamelessly hetero-sexual life, which was nonetheless fired and then kept on the rails by a contempt for anything girlish I detected in myself or in others. There were early feminists in my family. My step-grandmother and her sisters had tied themselves to the railings outside Holborn Post Office, and their mother joined them in prison to keep an eye on the catering and washing arrangements there. High heels and make-up, vanity and 'silliness', were looked at askance by these older women. 'Silliness', incidentally, was a word much used by the founder of Bedales in his writings on co-education, where it sat alongside other words like 'mawkish' and 'sentimental' as what sex could so easily become when girls and boys forgot to be 'sensible'. It was not only older women who poured scorn on all forms of vanity, however. The men in my family agreed with them. A painted woman was quite simply a woman too plain to get by without make-up, and who — by trying to rectify the position — made herself doubly abhorrent or anyway absurd. Such views worked to legislate unfairly, it seemed to me, against anyone who wanted to change their appearance, or, indeed, their accent.

When I was eighteen or so I attended a family party wearing modest court shoes, with what were known as Louis heels, and raspberry-pink lipstick — all this in order to try out what felt like a new and transvestite femininity. I remember a trio of midget great-aunts honking and spluttering with laughter as they contemplated the bedizened foolishness of their young relation. Of course, I may have been wearing my 'New Look' suit as well. This had been made from a length of brown-and-white herringbone tweed, sent, unrationed, from Ireland by a family friend. My mother had inherited from her stepmother a Miss Boutelle, or Miss Bottle, if you'd grown up watching her turn sheets 'sides to middle' during her annual, week-long visits, as my mother had. Miss Boutelle took particular pride, I remember, in cutting the greatest number of garments from the least possible amount of material, so it is entirely possible that I had a bag, waistcoat and even knickers to match. The suit 'skimmed', as they say these days, my adolescent body, before skidding violently in at the waist and then waywardly out again into what we all thought of as a 'peplum'. Even I knew that this was not a successful 'get-up'.

★　★　★

I should have been a natural for the women's movement of the late 1960s, but in fact this re-emerging feminism flustered me. Sisterhood and the celebration of women's lives: these were difficult ideas. I had three children by then and I worked first as a publisher and then as a teacher. I couldn't see my way, however, to celebrating my life or other women's lives, let alone our bodies or our bodily achievements, in language that could be spoken at all easily in mixed company. As far as I was concerned these were private pains and pleasures, which might occasionally and shamefacedly be touched upon with a single close friend, and for which I (like other women, I assumed) had no adequate language. I think I probably liked it that way, welcoming the silence, the squeamishness and the privacy. I know that I winced at some of the language of feminism, or its languages. I still do.

Things changed for me in the late 1970s — as they probably did for other women — as my children grew up and my professional work expanded. I was teaching in a university by then. I wrote a book about bilingualism and bilingual writers, and I learned about feminism from my women students, who were a generation younger than me, and from my reading. In 1984, I began work on a book called *Women Writing About Men*, which was mainly concerned with fiction, but which also considered language and the possibility that women were in some sense bilingual, though I meant this as a metaphor. I remember sitting at my desk, stuck for a beginning and a voice that would carry the ambiguity of what I wanted to write about the authority of interpretation, criticism, theory and my own relation to such activities. I was conscious, as who could help being, of the huge, padding, barefooted figure of one of my sons, who was at that point in his life when I simultaneously mourned his leaving home and wondered if he ever would. Then, eureka! A memory. Not, as it happens, of him, but of his older brother, who was born in 1957. It caught my dilemma exactly, the way I thought of myself, now and in the past, as a woman and a reader, though I left out the fact that I had chain-smoked Woodbine cigarettes throughout that time and in my long-suffering baby's face. 'Imagine,' I wrote,

> a young woman is suckling her son. As he wriggles from her into sudden, heavy sleep, milk spurts from her breast and on to the pages of Volume VII of Proust's *A la recherche du temps perdu*. She dabs the book with a muslin napkin, buttons herself, reads on, while her son sleeps. She is an obedient woman, a mother, a cleaner, an androgynous reader. When her son is older and has learned rhythmically to beat his custard-cream biscuit on the tray of his high chair, she steals moments to follow Saint-Loup with his regiment or the Baron de Charlus sidling past the concierge.

My son – the padder, not the feeder – was appalled. What possible connection could there be between breastfeeding and Proust? He'd given me the benefit of the doubt, believed I was writing a serious book: one his college supervisor or even his father might be prepared to read. I expect that I congratulated him in a teacherly way on his 'good' question, but it was dispiriting for both of us. I left that moment in, however, and it altered the course of the book. It altered me too, by allowing me to think about reading and literature not

as abstractions, but as always situated and embodied activities, in which women particularly may live out some of the contradictions of their lives. Readers lie on their beds or sit on the ground or in the nobly upholstered chairs of copyright libraries; or they feed their babies while turning the pages, sometimes in the middle of the night. Those moments made it possible to think of myself as multiple, as simultaneously mother/reader/writer, even critic, for those roles were performed by the same body, after all. This seemed to be a way of defying the destructive polarities of male and female, if only momentarily and for myself. I have thought of myself as a feminist ever since, though no doubt a feminist of a quite particular stamp and generation, and a good deal better (though not, of course, good enough) at analysis than revolution.

'Tomboys' were rude, boisterous and forward boys in the sixteenth century, before they were bold or immodest women, or girls who behave like spirited or boisterous boys, or wild romping girls or hoydens. I filch this history and these meanings of the word from the *Oxford English Dictionary*, and they interest me. There, sandwiched between the boys' rudeness and the boisterous romping hoyden, is the problem: the woman, whose boldness and immodesty unwoman her. My 'boyishness' as a young girl was defiantly not 'mannishness', I should add, a word I had heard used about friends of my parents and about aunts and teachers, who were unmarried. One was a farmer called Peter, who sold her produce in the market square on Saturday mornings. I feared becoming like Peter – though she was a handsome spectacle in her high leather boots and breeches – almost as much as I feared the equally menacing prospect of becoming an adult person at all.

Thinking of yourself as a tomboy may be one way of ducking your sexual future and all that is involved in judgements about children's likely performance as men or women; it is at any rate a delaying move, even a denial – though an all too provisional one – of the prospect of adulthood so ambiguously presented to children as crystal clear in its divisions, though it can also seem blurred by its secrets to the sepia indistinctness of an old photograph. From reading memoirs by women I get the sense that working-class girls are less likely to dread adult femininity in quite the way I did. Perhaps for women growing up in working-class families an acknowledgement and even a precocious assumption of adult female sexuality provide leverage for resistance to parental control, and even a prospect of possible power and pleasure at the pivotal centre of homes and families. It may also say something about the different ways in which childhood is valued that I should have wished to continue with mine, while some of my working-class contemporaries could hardly wait to escape from theirs.

I was eight when a small red-haired girl with freckles called Ray Burnett, who lived in the impoverished back-to-back terrace behind our house, told me how her mother's new baby had come to be born. This was, as it happens, at a moment when my own mother was expecting her third child. I knew for certain that Ray was wrong, that she had either made it up or been gullible to some crackpot theory deriving from her Scottish, Catholic and working-class family. It was characteristic that I should know more about class than sex at that point, I think. It was also clear to me that my parents would not have heard of these fantastical ideas. What indeed *had* they heard on the subject? I felt some compassion for them as they wallowed in what I believed to be total ignorance of how their soon-to-be three children had come into existence. So I did not challenge them for confirmation of Ray's unlikely tale. They'd have been shocked or upset, I thought, by such nonsense. But I pondered the implications, which were on the whole worrying ones.

Between the ages of eight and twelve, when my first period drove me to lock myself in my room for two whole days in an effort to ignore my body and its awful leakages, while reading *Forever Amber* on my bed, I think of myself as living in a state of perpetual and contrary motion. I built houses in trees and dug tunnels for escape and graves for pets and deep hollows for swimming pools. I begin to see that assembling my mother's monumental art school paintings into a small wigwam of my own in our attic and letting that candle burn down the top floor of the house was just one of a series of auto-didactic 'projects'. I dropped the black and white baby dolls I loved from the top of the stairs to the bottom, so that their round, bald heads cracked open, and then I tenderly ministered to them with TCP and sticking plaster. I read school stories by P. G. Wodehouse and dreamed of firing popguns and climbing out of Gothic windows and shinning down the ivy-clad walls of a boys' boarding school.

It does seem possible that at the heart of heterosexual middle-class culture in the Western world is a shared dislike and distrust of women: shared, that is, by men and women. I remember being warned that there were some grown-up men who had designs on girls like me, and feeling and expressing incredulity at such a thought. There was nothing about my body I could imagine anyone having designs on. I suppose I was one of those girls who internalise a generalised contempt for the female, perhaps as a consequence of disappointment. The love that may have been lavished on us as very small children is later called into question by the recognition that we are, after all, girls and will become women. The first object of this newly learned contempt may be our own mother, that interloper between father and daughter, that reminder that the daughter is, after all, a daughter and not a surrogate son. As an oldest child and daughter,

I convinced myself that my father preferred me to his wife, and that his doing so depended in some measure on my similarity to him, on my boyishness. Nor was I altogether wrong. My father certainly transmitted double messages. He may have liked me as a tomboy, but it troubled him too. Yet I knew that he regarded conventionally feminine behaviour as trivial and time-wasting, and he made no allowances for women's incapacity to walk as fast as he could or to carry heavy weights. Nor did I ever feel that he responded positively to female beauty, though he was quick to notice its absence.

My mother was not feminine in conventional ways. Despite her good looks and though she was a painter she showed absolutely no interest in decorating her house, her face or her body, for instance. Yet I grew up thinking of her as possessed of some of those feminine weaknesses I particularly dreaded finding in myself: dithering, soppiness and ignorance were among the worst of these. She also sent out double messages: that looks mattered, that girls who worked too hard for their exams might lose such looks as they had and come a cropper. And she conveyed to her daughters that there really was something to be said for getting married, despite the snags, if only to make it easier to get on with what you wanted to do in life. Sometimes she wondered wistfully whether friendships with women might have delivered greater happiness.

I think of both my parents as living with a more or less suppressed interest in members of their own sex, and I think of my growing up as plagued by a constant, but perhaps quite unexceptional, nagging at questions of sexual identity and allegiance, questions which were never clearly articulated, let alone answered. Given my parents' own ambivalences it is surprising that I experienced the family as so firmly and inexorably directing me towards living my life as a heterosexual woman, indeed towards what Adrienne Rich once called 'compulsory heterosexuality'. I must have been exposed to a good deal less coercion than most girls of my generation were.

Thinking of yourself as a tomboy was a way of being neither my mother nor my father nor, indeed, any adult, and so it was a way of staying young and avoiding guilt; and like most children, I had an interest in doing that. It was also a way of skirting certainty, decisiveness, clarity, of embracing ambiguity; and only now, in old age, can I see how important that has been. The pains of not belonging contained their own compensation. Having a Jewish mother and an English and vestigially Unitarian father meant that I had no need to be what they were or a hundred other things besides. *Not* being things offers real comforts and consolations, and I was especially *not* going to be any kind of artist. I've found the idea of negative capability and of the hybrid infinitely appealing, though like most children I homed in on the magnet lure of various forms of normality and acceptability, and often wished to participate in whatever they happened to be. It may even have been that my tomboy status provided me with a refuge from the harsher antagonisms and separations of class. Ray Burnett's parents, for instance, thought me a bad influence rather than posh. And I had a pretext other than class for distancing myself from the games she played with her sisters and friends, dressed in their mother's shoes and pinafores, alternately rocking and chastising their dolls.

The terrifying certainties of 1970s feminism rattled me all over again with their threat that I should be required to declare myself a paid-up woman, who was pleased and proud to be one. It was common in my youth to speak of the occasional woman as having a man's mind, and so long as everything else about her was properly feminine this might be considered an egregious compliment. So I could no more glory in my female mind than in my female body. Both were porous and occasioned shame. Nor could I ally myself straightforwardly with groups of women rather than particular ones. I have occasionally asked my women friends how they came to reconcile themselves to a future as women. Did they not sometimes react with a start of amazement to the realisation that the whole of their lives would be spent as members of the second sex? Most of them have been surprised to be asked such a question. They had not, by and large, accepted the superiority of the male as literally as I had.

Yet feminism as a politics and an analysis has been powerful and inspiring. Not because it has delivered happiness to women or reversed the power structures of this society or any other, or even because it has argued for the difference and the validity of women's lives and against those injustices that have made them worse than they needed to be, though there have, after all, been some successes on all these fronts. Perhaps the main benefit of feminism for me has been that it started, *faute de mieux*, from outside, from the illuminating double vision of the excluded, the oppressed, the colonised and the subaltern, and then moved towards exposure of the quaint and appalling grimness of certain established, confident ways of life, which are likely to be thought of as natural, neutral, normal and even as universal, transcendent, beyond criticism.

Feminism's questions have had the potential to unsettle complacency and the accepted, and have even begun to dismantle some of society's most rooted and cherished certainties: about sex and family life and language, for instance. They have done so from a position which exposes and then exploits the double character of women's inclusion in social arrangements. As daughters or sisters or wives or mothers, women may be so protected and sanctified as to disguise the reality of their effective exclusion from public discourse, from the means of determining what is and what matters. At the same

time, women's traditional roles may in their material lives constitute the site of their greatest vulnerability, even as public discourse reassuringly announces their equal status as citizens, workers, consumers. Feminism has also had to reckon with the sheer seductiveness of power, and with the ways in which women have come to be seduced by power as well as by men, by their ideas and bodies and texts and arguments, into agreement and into forms of androgyny.

It seems right to be suspicious of any life narrative which coheres round assumptions of human consistency or the integrity and continuity of the self. The sense I had of myself as a mutinous tomboy persisted into adolescence and, in some ways, beyond. I was often in love with boys, but from a distance, likely to be off at the first sign of reciprocated devotion, let alone any possibility that it might be acted upon. I was adamantly unreceptive to the character of boys' interest in girls, because I guessed, I suppose, that some boys did respond to the 'girlish' in girls, and that was not to be borne. I knew why Jo March, whom I admired unreservedly at one time, rejected Laurie in *Little Women* and why Amy married him. I also knew from my reading that if you dropped your guard with boys you might sink into a state of apparent dependence on them, which they couldn't handle. And of course I have sometimes dropped my guard, and learned that, just as I'd thought, it doesn't work. Even as I read my way through books I thought of as 'slushy' rubbish (two a day from the local library during one summer holiday), I knew that I was grateful for these authors' haziness about the nature of both sexual attraction and the sexual act itself, and for the particular

93

truth of that to women's doubleness: that they could want men's love but also covet men's power to confer, to refuse or to enact it.

Leo Bersani writes about that apparent contradiction in his book *Homos*, both as it characterises same-gender desire and as it is reflected in the struggles of heterosexual men and women to accommodate another's attractions, when their sheer difference from our own, whatever they may be, must inevitably cast some doubt on such alien charms.

If this means that the desire to have is never entirely distinct from the desire to be, the boundaries between having and being are bound to be more blurred in same-gender desire than in heterosexual desire. The former *begins* with a recognition of sameness; the latter includes (and struggles to overcome) the memory of a traumatic encounter with difference. In his desires, the gay man always runs the risk of identifying with culturally dominant images of misogynist maleness. For the sexual drives of gay men do, after all, extend beyond the rather narrow circle of other politically correct gay men. A more or less secret sympathy with heterosexual male misogyny carries with it the narcissistically gratifying reward of confirming our membership in (and not simply our erotic appetite for) the privileged male society.

Bersani says that women's ambiguous feelings about men have something in common with those of male homosexuals, who are drawn in some cases to the misogyny embedded in heterosexual culture, precisely *because* it excludes them.

Throughout my adolescence I read – as well as other things – women's magazines and the peculiar wartime romances of the 1940s, in which uniformed couples embraced one another on windy hilltops to the sound of an air-raid warning, passionately admitting to the impossibility of achieving sexual satisfaction. I wanted to read about sexual desire, but I was mightily relieved by what seemed to be its inevitable frustration. I liked love to nestle safely within regulation and constraint, the agreement to hold back. I have not felt able to read stories like that for more than fifty years now, and when I look back on them from here it seems that they begin from women's disappointment with men, with men's failure to hear, understand, sympathise. And then, as the plot picks up, there is scope for the woman to persuade the man on to her side, to tame him, transform him to the familiar man of her fantasies, the one who recognises her as a soulmate, a sister, a tomboy: his adored masculinity tempered and tampered with, and translated into a form the woman reader can tolerate or even emulate. A bad man transformed on the stroke of midnight into a good mother: that was the romance for me.

While talking about these things recently with my daughter – whose own eight-year-old daughter surmised wearily the other day that sex seemed from where she stood to be 'a long and difficult process', probably not worth the candle – she told me that her plan to dismember her brother had, in fact, been short-lived. She had thought better of it and asked him instead to make her a wooden penis in the carpentry classes available to boys in their school but not to girls. An altogether more practical proposal. She doesn't remember his reply.

★   ★   ★

95

It is not always easy to recognise oneself in childhood memories, and yet here I am looking to them for themes, links, starting points. I have an intermediate memory, though; one that connects what Emma Tennant has called 'girlitude' with adulthood, a bridge between my awkward tomboy tactics and the blushing subterfuges of the briefly nubile young woman I must once have been. I am at university. I mostly think of Cambridge as damp: damp walls, wet grass, dark skies, tears. Yet I can make myself feel the elegiac warmth of late September, when, at the beginning of my third and last year there, in 1954, I went back early, before term. There was a small commotion in my college, I remember. A handsome American woman, a rare postgraduate, from Vassar or Bryn Mawr, had sent her car and jewels ahead of her, by sea. Mysteriously, they had not arrived. The few of us in the building were called to the library and questioned sleepily by the police. Back in my new room, strewn with cups and books and a kettle retrieved from summer storage, I muttered crossly to myself about cars and jewels and what did she think she'd do with such things here anyway. My room was graced by six high barred windows, and one bar had been neatly sawn through, so that the room provided the best way into college for anyone who came back late, after the main doors had closed. My room was pretty, despite its bars, and popular with mice. Having moved my desk to a rakish slant across one corner of the room and casually settled a full bottle of rum on the mantelpiece above the popping gas fire, I left for town.

G2, in one of the men's colleges, a cluttered pair of rooms facing inward to a small courtyard hung with Virginia creeper, was shared by two friends. One, for most of the time elegantly prone, was later and with some ignominy diagnosed as suffering from too much sleep, not too much sin, as he'd hoped. The other, his slight squint trained on next year and London, arose each day at six to get started on his letters of apology and applications for jobs. The dull blue curtains were drawn against the autumn sun. A typewriter clattered in the bedroom, and light groans issued from my friend on his back as he gauged the temperature of the day from the sounds of footsteps outside. Three more friends came in. Someone had brought a bottle of wine, someone else some beer. This year was to be a special one for us all, it was agreed; a year when pleasure would prevail, when wit, laughter and many varieties of bad behaviour would reach new heights of creative refinement. We would be Falstaffian. Might we not indeed constitute ourselves as the Falstaff Society, dedicated to excess and friendship and literature and, above all, to sexual intercourse? There would be no more restraint, cowardice, inhibitions. We would have no time for the drearily authoritarian, the pettily anxious, the abjectly obedient, and so on and on. Someone read aloud from *Henry IV, Part I*:

> Marry then, sweet wag, when thou art king, let not us that are squires of the night's body be called thieves of the day's beauty; let us be Diana's foresters, gentlemen of the shade, minions of the moon, and let men say we be men of good government, being governed as the sea is by our noble and chaste mistress the moon, under whose countenance we steal.

Unwisely, I asked if I was to be Diana in all this, or just another of her foresters. Perhaps I could be a wag. 'Oh, there are parts for you,' someone airily replied, 'Mistress Quickly, Doll Tearsheet.'

My question, easily read from here as spoilsport, spoiled nothing. The society would need more women, and others who would be back in a week were considered. I blushed at my uneasiness, hoped I'd got the joke and might even make a few myself if I could get a word in edgeways. A sense of humour (the 'h' sometimes stylishly dropped) was mandatory for playmates. The euphoria of that particular day evaporated, though its memory conjures up other times. 'Panache' was a favourite word, and 'dressed only in his panache' was how a friend's scaling of King's College Chapel, in his socks and in the dead of night, came to be told.

It is not by any means that memories like these are sad ones, nor do I feel inclined to relinquish or disown them. They are as much a part of my youth as they are part of the youth of those young men who were, admittedly, more likely than I was to figure heroically in them. But I am taunted by their ambiguity, and I still think of them somehow as riddles. There is my uncertain membership of a group already so adept at its own narrative and so clear about the traditions and lineage impinging on that narrative. Several of my male contemporaries have written of that time, of the river's banks and college 'backs', of bikes and Mill Lane and the Eagle pub, where double helixes were at that very moment being sketched out among the crisps and crumbs, of friends who were poets, and supervisors who became your friends, of a secret society, even of girls or dreams of girls, though many of the men also dreamed of each other. All these reminiscences are full of jokes and revelations of a kind to be understood as presaging later achievements or surprises.

It may be significant that I fix on a moment before term began, when, as it happened, I was the only woman in this group of men. Perhaps I need to separate myself like that, to avoid speaking for other – let alone all – women students of my generation. Certainly my sense of difference and isolation was not at all straightforwardly shared by my women friends, and anyway our relations with men could characteristically cut us off from one another in this world remembered unequivocally as golden by so many of the men in it. The young woman with whom I have to identify in a whole sequence of scenes is hard to fathom. I think of her cringing from her own duplicity, ashamed of the sheer accomplishment of her quizzical glance, running from invitations and from the impossible demands they made on wit and

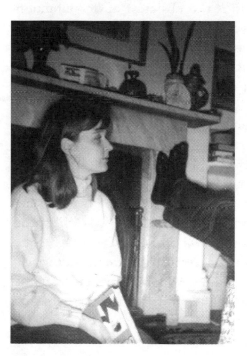

wardrobe. Then I am embarrassed by the thought that this young woman was in some way desired by one or more of the men in the group, that she knew this, that her head and senses were flushed with the thought of it. And though, of course, she'd have wanted to claim an additional history and purpose to her presence there, an awkward honesty would have made both quite difficult to pinpoint.

I am beginning to think that I am missing from my own memories as I try to focus on that smudged glimpse of a young woman, who was, in 1954, starting her final year as a student of French and Russian at an ancient British university. Can I hope to watch, let alone inhabit, the body of that young woman nearly fifty years ago, given the history that has always found it easy to dispose of her testimony? And what would that testimony have contained anyway? Pleasure? Desire? Whose pleasure and desire? A sense of time, perhaps, of a moment holding what might become of us all? Was it ever *not* the pleasure and desire of others that she knew about? And what *was* the pleasure in the strange chance of knowing herself only as the object of others' intentions and momentary covetousness? Her eyes seem too open and shining. She was learning to guard against displays of innocence or ignorance, though a few years later her husband would still have to remind her to put on her arrogant face as they wait for their hosts to open the door and usher them in. What could she have said in defence of her essay on *Anna Karenina* to the brusque military man who ordered his male students to their feet when she arrived, late, for his lecture? Cambridge was a city of men. She was welcome here so long as she laughed and danced for them in the ways literature assured them women could and did. Let her beware, though, of asking for quarter in the examinations hall or of asserting her difference from them in ways that might seem to question their absolute right to be where they were.

Just six years earlier, in 1948, the women's colleges had

finally been granted full membership of the university, though women had studied there since 1869. When I was at Cambridge women students were still in a ratio of one to ten men, so that, as a history of my old college drily puts it, young women 'were in constant demand to sing, act, or simply be escorted to parties and dances'. We were also in some demand as possible members of a dreamed-up Falstaff Society bent, above all, on continuous sexual intercourse.

The inequalities and anomalies were not, of course, intolerable, nor were they much discussed. We knew that most of our contemporaries (male as well as female) still left school at fourteen to start work. A few girls stayed on beyond fourteen to study art or domestic science – in preparation for marriage, as some would have put it. The majority of the girls I knew stayed at school until they were seventeen or eighteen and then trained as teachers or nurses or secretaries. In fact, the first thing I did on leaving university was learn to type and do shorthand, in a class full of seventeen-year-olds doing both things much better than I ever would. There was a realistic expectation that even with a degree I would need to take some man's dictation before long if I was to get on in life. Most young women of my age in 1954 had far more to complain about than I had, and, such were the times, I expect they complained far less. For the contradictions inherent in my position as a young woman student in an ancient and originally monastic institution are only one aspect of the contradictions which have persistently dogged the education of girls during the last 150 years – and they dog it still, even in this era of girls outdoing boys in examinations.

The education on offer at Cambridge when I was

there relied on the assumption that, whereas men were always and everywhere simply men, women were women for only some of the time. In our reading, our writing, in lectures and seminars and examinations, we were expected to drop whatever being a woman might mean to us or to others and to become as like men as we could – or at least flexibly androgynous. Such a division of ourselves often felt quite comfortable, since even those of us whose schooling had been in all-female institutions (as most of mine had not) were accustomed to the uneasy settlement entailed in joining the 'we' of science textbooks, historical researchers, critics or philosophers. We had learned to perform this trick during the last years of our schooling, and we learned it just as boys did, as one of all those other tricks which potential university students master in order to announce their worldliness, omniscience and detachment.

Inevitably, though, there were difficulties. It was not only the fact of our bodies, our biological difference from men, that was cancelled out by such manoeuvres. Many of our past and current preoccupations were also ruled irrelevant. And then these separated parts of ourselves refused at times to stay separate, particularly if the work we were doing was in anthropology or history or literature. All three are, after all, crammed with women. The problem there is with who undertakes to tell us about them and how we, as serious students, might ourselves think and talk about women and who they are. Sweet girl graduate or '*Was will das Weib?*', playmate or arcane subject matter, allegedly requiring the most rigorous of psychological or sociological methodologies? For some of us there were actually one or two writers on the syllabus who were women – not many, but some;

and we were quite often taught by women as well. But if women writers and scholars were to be worthy of our respect, it became all the more necessary to shed our own gender and theirs in any evaluation we might make of their work.

What I am remembering is a particular form of induction into the way things were done in universities in Britain in particular subject areas and at a particular time. For young people in universities the modes of teaching and learning and the accepted styles of written and spoken language constitute an induction into knowledge, but also into forms of knowing and showing that you know. Examinations at the end of it all validate the rightness of all these procedures against any single student's objections to them. Many women writers have recalled the devastating loss of confidence dealt them by these traditions, from which not only women but sexual difference had, by definition, been expunged. In returning to that time in my own life, I realise that I accepted without demur what seemed like a requirement to read and write and think in two entirely different ways. For many years I believed that you should not include anything you actually thought or felt in an essay. It is possible that when I wrote about *Anna Karenina* I let some cat out of the bag, which accounts for my memory of having somehow discomfited my soldierly supervisor in Russian literature. I know now, of course, that it was naive of me to take to heart with quite such energy a diffuse set of injunctions to be sophisticated at all costs, to stick with the 'passive' and the impersonal – 'one is obliged to conclude that' and so on – and never to make too much of my own predilections. All this certainly managed to empty my studies of interest for a time, though it also taught me that schooling sets itself the task of initiating the young into just such divisions and separations, and that the best teachers see it as their job to share that insight with those they teach, if only to enable them to circumvent it.

Miss Collet

My mother used to wonder why anyone would want to write about my great-aunt Clara rather than her sisters, Caroline and Edith, who were so much nicer, and there is no easy answer to that. All three were my father's aunts, and they had brought him up. Clara was the second daughter and fourth of the five children of Collet Dobson Collet, campaigner for a free press, singer, editor of little magazines and author of a history of the campaign to abolish the newspaper tax, and his wife Jane, who owned and ran a laundry in North London. The laundry must have supported the family, though her husband sang in the chorus at Covent Garden, and that would have brought in something. They were also neighbours and friends of Karl Marx, whose youngest daughter Eleanor was much doted on as an enviably older adolescent by the fierce young Clara. Only a few people called her Clara, in fact. She was Miss Collet to all who knew her outside the family, and even the novelist George Gissing, who wrote to her regularly for ten years, never called her anything but Miss Collet.

She was born in 1860 and died after the Second World War in 1948. I remember her as small, neat and formidable, with an impressive double chin and chilly ways. She once asked me what I meant to do when I grew up and was horrified to learn that I wanted first to be an Olympic diver and thereafter a PE teacher. I was no

better pleased with her answer to my question: what, I wanted to know, would happen after their deaths to all that she and her sisters and brother absorbed from the two books a day delivered to their door by a van from the local library? 'Nothing will happen,' was her irritable reply, 'absolutely nothing whatever.'

My few visual memories of Aunt Clara are as precise and brisk as she was. I catch her walking rapidly from room to room in a large wooden bungalow, edged on three sides by a deep veranda and perched on the dangerously sheer and unfenced cliffs of Sidmouth in Devon. As the member of what was left of her immediate family with the best pension and the greatest experience of the world, she had moved them all there from Hampstead in 1936. In the big square room on one side of the house, with its mahogany bookcases and its grand piano, four card tables were set as far apart from each other as possible. Here, during the last years of their long lives, Carrie, the eldest, Harold, the second son, and Edith, the baby, sat at their books and newspapers and their Patience and

Solitaire, inwardly railing, perhaps, at the high-handed way in which Clara had transported them there. She had gone to Sidmouth for short holidays all her adult life, and on one particular September visit it had seemed to her 'like heaven here, a balmy, sleepy and invigorating heaven!' She decided at once, as she was given to doing, that they must leave London, sell up and buy a house here. She had already put a deposit on the house she wanted before proposing the move to her sisters and brother. Harold replied mournfully to her seductive account of Sidmouth's golf links and other charms, 'Your letter is rather terrifying to me, it was so wholly un-expected and upsetting. I suppose I shall get used to the notion gradually, but at present I cannot get my ideas together.' He wondered who would manage the nine houses in Finsbury Park they let and lived off, and reminded his sister that he was far too old for golf and for making new friends. But you could not hold out for long against Clara, it seems. Less than a year later, she had a breast removed by Geoffrey Keynes, brother of Maynard and expert on William Blake: an unusual sur-geon, not least for writing to his patient after the oper-ation to find out how she was and to congratulate her on taking it all so philosophically.

I don't think I understood about change or growing old or even about the past in those days, and I assumed that these four old people had always been as they were when I knew them. Aunt Carrie had always worn her hair in a thin plait at night, and her long white cotton nightie might have been the one she had as a child, just as she had always dressed during the day in rustling black silk at least fifty years (perhaps a hundred) out of date, with a silver chatelaine for her pince-nez clipped to her belt. I was sure that Aunt Edith's mind had always sweetly wandered and that she had always found dressing a confusing affair, and that Uncle Harold had always sat smiling and nervous among his cricket and golf mementoes, with apparently nothing to do. It was not possible for me to imagine him as a good-looking young man who actually used these things. And Aunt Clara had always been bossy and worn grey stockings and what was called a navy coat and skirt. I never bothered to wonder how their older brother Wilfred had fitted in. He was my grandfather and would have been nearly as old as Carrie, but he had died before I was born. My sisters and I liked dressing up in his uniforms and trailing his gloriously gold-braided trousers behind us as we tore round our muddy garden. You got the impression he had been a pretty stout gentleman, whose girth made up for his lack of height. Not at all like his youngest son.

Most of my father's memories of his aunts were of their late forties, perhaps their prime. He was a late child. His mother died when he was five, and as his father was away for most of the time, governing the least glamorous of Britain's colonies, his aunts and uncle brought him up, occasionally galvanised into taking his photograph or buying him new clothes by demands from their absent and bill-paying brother. Harold sent some photographs of my father to Edith during the war, when she was away from home, and wrote, 'Clara does not think them perfectly sweet, but rather ghastly, and calculated to give Wilf a bad turn if he sees them.' In fact, it was Edith who mainly brought my father up, and he loved her the most by far. Clara was not always there and did not suffer fools gladly, and Carrie had 'poor health' of a mysterious kind: a hysterical kind, perhaps, brought on by the arrival of two younger sisters. It was her convalescing there that had introduced the family to Sidmouth in the first place. She also had a demanding friend called Miss Bolus – Fanny Bolus, in fact, whose name my father could never utter without a giggle. Both Clara and Carrie occasionally boasted about their small nephew to their friends behind his back. For them, he was something of 'a wonder child'.

In 1910 Clara wrote in her diary:

> On the 2nd June I sent in my resignation for two reasons (1) in order to speak freely about the way in which the women's side of the Labour Exchanges is being organised, capable women being subordinated to men who know nothing & care nothing about women's interests and (2) because there was nothing to stay for.

She was nearly fifty when she wrote that and seriously contemplated truncating a successful career as Senior Investigator at the Board of Trade. In the end she was persuaded to stay for another seven years. Her two reasons for wanting to resign carry some of the doubleness of her career. First, she felt that her professional and public position inhibited her speaking 'freely' as a woman, especially about issues of paramount importance to women, like wages. In 1891, Clara had been one of four women asked by the Royal Commission on Labour to report on women's 'sweating'. H. J. Mundella, the head of that commission, became President of the Board of Trade the following year and at once appointed Clara to a post as Labour Correspondent with special responsibility for women's industrial conditions.

Hilda Martindale, in her history of women civil servants, describes how Clara's department grew steadily, in line with increasing attention to women's work, so that before long she was allowed to appoint her own assistant investigator. For four years running, each of the four clever young women she recruited had to leave, as each one married and was forced by the marriage bar to abandon her job. By 1903, Clara had at last acquired a woman assistant who did not fall foul of the marriage bar, and had herself become a recognised expert on statistics. Clara was a rare bird, a woman civil servant, working with men, in institutions organised by men and for men and according to male traditions of professional behaviour and procedures. Yet her specialism was women's work, women's education and training, and women's pay.

During the thirty or so most active years of her professional life, between 1890 and the early 1920s, Clara lived as an unmarried man in her position might have done: sometimes with her family, more often alone in rooms, 'chambers' or flats, at first rented, but by the end of her working life, owned. She belonged to clubs and spent a good deal of her time on the committees of professional and academic associations. She was a founder member of the Committee of the Economic Club and of the councils of both the Royal Statistical Society and the Royal Economic Society. At different periods of her life she was President of the Association of Assistant Mistresses and a governor of Bedford College for Women in London. She may have been proudest of being the first woman to be made a fellow of University College London.

Clara belonged to a generation of active, intelligent middle-class women, many of them born, as she was, into Unitarian families, who, during the last thirty years of the nineteenth century and the first decades of the twentieth, were professionally involved in public life and particularly with the problems of urban poverty. But whereas Beatrice Potter was able to assure Sidney Webb in 1891 that she had an income of £1,500 a year, on which they might live, Clara always expected to earn her own living. She was never paid as much as her male colleagues, probably never more than £400 a year, but she was always financially independent and she enjoyed giving friends and relations small gifts and treats and occasional loans. She had, as she might have put it, 'done well for a woman'. Yet she remained subordinate to men less expert than she was in her field, just as her specialism would always be subordinate to questions about men's work and men's wages. And although she was one of a handful of women whose career offered some security and a pension, her entry into the Civil Service, and her position within it, remained outside the established career routes, and there was no possibility for her of promotion, or of mobility within the Service.

It is clear from her diaries that she thought often, if guardedly, about the difference between her life as a working woman and the life of a wife. Her professional preoccupations were with the class, economic and educational aspects of women's lives. She came to believe that middle-class women had, by marrying, committed themselves to wasting any training and professional qualifications they had in order to be wives and mothers. She may also have felt, exasperatedly, that it was the duty of married women who were not poor to withdraw

from competition for the kinds of jobs which were becoming available to women at the end of the nineteenth century.

She often registered her sense of the oddness of being a woman among men. For these were men married to women, and wives were translated by marriage to a sphere from which she, as an unmarried woman, was excluded. This was not always a painful matter. Indeed, she was often amused as she contemplated her colleagues' wives. On one of her extra-curricular committees, for instance, she met as its treasurer a Lady Dudley, who had come

straight from Paris to the Ctte. She was in a light gray dress that looked very summery near our dark dresses although I suppose it was merely her

travelling dress. She spoke very prettily to me afterwards saying that her husband was a colleague of
mine; that he said he had never seen me but he
was always interested in my work. She reads the
Labour Gazette right through. She evidently means
to make her husband a success.

Wives may have been capable of showing an interest
in public issues – may even have been genuinely well
versed in them – but as wives they became for a woman
like Clara pampered and patronising, and fair game for
her own condescension, which she permitted herself on
the grounds that these were women who had opted for
being useful primarily to her male colleagues.

All her life, Clara sought – and enjoyed – friendships
with men. In her twenties and early thirties it seems
likely that she thought of these (proudly and privately)
in relation to a possible marriage. Later, she wrote to
men who interested her, sending them things she had
written or telling them what she thought of their work.
Several responded enthusiastically: Israel Zangwill (an
admirer, as it happens, of Nina, my Jewish grandmother)
was one, Ramsay MacDonald another. Between 1909
and 1911 she received a dozen or so letters of great
charm and eccentricity from Edward Spencer, a free
spirit or early hippie, who ran a William Morris-like
craft business and had lively views about how to organise
workers and art and children. 'The worst of friendships
with men,' Clara wrote in her diary, 'is that one can't
cultivate them for any length of time; they must simply
come up & die without any attempt being made to
water them.' She envied 'George Eliot for her friendship with George Lewes', and must have meant that she

wished for a friendship with a man which was not always lived in the shadow of the man's marriage to another woman. Such equanimity as she expressed – if that is what it was – about men loving and marrying other women, and about the kinds of friendship it was possible for her to have with men and their wives, was won painfully. If she was once able to assert that a woman might possibly escape 'being old maidish by coming into daily contact with men professors and students', her capacity to identify with men in their sexual relations with women could relegate her to a position of uncomfortable asexuality, which might be as cheerfully exploited by women as by men.

She began her investigative career with Charles Booth and his 'Survey of London Life and Labour' in 1887 or 1888 and she became a close friend of Booth's remarkable wife Mary, who was probably one of the few women Clara knew who managed to bring up a large family of children, remain happily married and involve herself seriously and professionally in all aspects of her husband's work – his business as well as his vast investigative project. For years Mary and Clara wrote to each other about their lives and work and their political differences.

Compared with a slightly older cohort of women (her sister Carrie, for instance, who was five years older), Clara was fortunate. She was only in her eighteenth year in 1878 when London University approved the admission of women to degrees on the same terms as men. This opened up a wider set of professional possibilities for women who wanted a career outside teaching. Whereas contemporaries like Beatrice Webb were more or less educated within and by their families, Clara had been taught very well at school, and besides being a qualified

secondary school teacher had a BA and later an MA
from University College London.

Her diary began on 10 September 1876, her sixteenth
birthday, for which she received small bits of jewellery
and five books, most of them by women. She went to
Unitarian chapel that day and did 'nothing in the afternoon and the same in the evening'. The nearly two years
of her diary until she left school in the summer of 1878
to become a teacher herself are filled with family and
friends, with her reading, with school and exams and
with an anxiously glimpsed future beyond all this. She
is funny, confident and iconoclastic, precocious in her
determination to develop a style and wit for herself which
will eschew cant and – her *bête noire* – sentimentality.

Her family are the source of good times and presents. They are also ridiculous, and the male members have inherited a reprehensible saintliness. She is not fond of good boys. There are visits to the theatre, and the family is musical. Her brother Wilfred is inclined to talk 'a lot of bosh', particularly about young women. But he has his points, especially when he arranges Shakespeare evenings. These are sometimes at the Collet home, Sunny Bank, which also housed the family's laundry and was set in the middle of the fields that lay between Archway and Hornsey Rise; and sometimes at the Marxes' house in Maitland Park Road, Kentish Town. Eleanor Marx (Tussy to her family and friends) is marvellous as Rosalind and 'perfect' as Lady Anne in *Richard III*. She is five years older than Clara and secretly engaged to the

Frenchman always known as Lissagaray, of whom Marx disapproves. This was presumably to do with his age (he was seventeen years older than Eleanor), because Marx went to considerable lengths in the 1880s to support the publication of Lissagaray's *History of the Commune of 1871*, when Eleanor was translating it into English. Sixteen-year-old Clara can't wait for Tussy to return from Carlsbad, where she's been with her father. And when she does come back, the younger girl is grandly impatient with Lissa, as she conspiratorially calls him, for monopolising her friend. 'He is not half good enough for her.' Perhaps, she muses, he might 'commit forgery & suicide'. The Shakespeare play-readings are formalised. Clara records the establishing of the Dogberry Club in August 1877 and a reading of *The Merchant of Venice* in November of that year. The Maitland girls, Dolly and Clara, Tussy's friends originally, as well as several less acceptable male members of the Maitland family, join the club too. Clara is intrigued by the young men she meets, though also defensively critical of their looks, their brains, their tendency to extreme conceit and to discussing topics on which they are ill-informed. She is highly entertained by a young man seen waving to his wife from the train as it passes her window. Such attentiveness to a wife who is still in bed when her husband leaves for work is absurd, unwarranted and unlikely to last.

Occasionally, Clara goes to bed early because there is nothing left to read. She records vast and eclectic reading, from children's books to philosophy. After reading a life of Byron she announces, 'He was bad but he is the only person that I ever loved (whom I am not personally acquainted with). I hate his prim prig of a wife with all my heart & all my soul.' She responds to the story of a daughter voluntarily joining her father in Botany Bay, 'Catch me going to Botany Bay for anybody unless myself.' She will never of her own free will 'read a single page of that detestable hound Leigh Hunt'. Years later she will excoriate in similar style his neighbour, Thomas Carlyle, 'who cared nothing for fine art, and never discovered ability in anyone who did not first pay homage to himself'. Even Florence Nightingale, whom Clara had once admired, wrote 'sickening letters'. John Stuart Mill was 'dull & no mistake', though she later wrote enthusiastically of his generosity and love of truth. She is impressed by a sermon she hears on the sixteenth-century Protestant martyr Anne Askew, in which it was suggested that she was 'not bad for a woman'. She reads and loves the novels of Elizabeth Gaskell and Charlotte Brontë, and is delighted by Gaskell's biography of Charlotte. One criterion for judging a book is for what it offers 'the female portion of the world', and it may be failure on that front which provokes her condemnation of Goethe's autobiography, 'the most conceited book I ever read . . . the man himself is disgusting'. George Lewes's life of Goethe is far better, and by the end of it even Goethe has somewhat redeemed himself in her eyes.

Aunt Sophia (Sophy), her father's sister, is a favourite of Clara's and a writer, who corresponded with Maria Edgeworth and knew Emerson in her youth. She has stories of Emerson's to tell about Louisa Alcott. It seems that the Alcotts were most satisfactorily like the March family in *Little Women* and *Good Wives*. 'Mr Alcott was always talking about celibacy as though everyone ought to practise it. His wife got so sick of hearing him talk

about it that she left him. Mr Alcott bore it for one day
and then fetched her back.' And 'Emerson used to put
a bank note into Alcott's desk or some place where he
would be sure to find it, when Alcott was hard up.
Neither of them said anything about it to each other.'

School is interesting, Clara writes in her diary, though
it is not allowed to take up too much of her time. Girls
who take more than three hours to do their homework
must be 'duffers'. She is doing chemistry, physics and
maths, but she is best at English, French, German, Latin
and philosophy. Her school was the North London
Collegiate School, founded in 1850 by the ardent and
capable Frances Mary Buss, who seems to have taken a
kindly interest in Clara. Indeed, she wrote to Clara's great-
aunt Mary, another teacher, to tell her that her niece
had 'distinguished herself in school – she is a clever girl,
and works well. I think from present appearances Edith
will follow in her sister's footsteps.' Clara, like her brothers
and sisters, spent a year at a Catholic boarding school in
France before starting at North London, which offered
a broader and probably better taught curriculum than
the majority of boys' public schools at the time and
encouraged the maximum academic ambition in its
pupils, despite the relatively exiguous prospects awaiting
them.

There are visits to museums and plays. One to the
South Kensington Museum is 'dreadfully instructive': the
only really interesting exhibit a 'machine for measuring
the intensity of thought'. Her favourite teacher, Miss
Oswald, is shocked that Clara does not admire Goethe's
Hermann und Dorothea and regards as 'something fearful'
her 'want of poetic appreciation'. Clara and two other
girls have statistics lessons with a Dr Aveling – the same

Edward Aveling with whom her friend Eleanor Marx will spend the last years of her life, for the most part unhappily. Clara thinks about becoming a writer, but there is always the risk of making yourself ridiculous, though that is a fate that no one she knows is much good at avoiding. There is the associated hazard of self-consciousness, one of the problems with diaries:

> The worst of a diary is that when anything happens you have no time to write about it, when you have time nothing happens . . . I have come to the conclusion that if I ever wish to write anything worth writing I ought to make note of my own thoughts & opinions more than I have done; it will give me ease in writing and provided I do it truthfully it will be amusing to compare changing opinions. The most difficult thing in a diary is to write totally for yourself; try as hard as one will there is always the *arrière-pensée* about what people would think if they read it.

Clara wrote her diary from the beginning with some such thought in mind. She alludes more than once to having omitted painful events on the grounds that she is unlikely to forget them and they would be of no interest to anyone else. Later, she destroyed the section of her diary which coincided with a crisis in her friendship with George Gissing. She even edited a version of the diary she wrote during her seven years teaching in Leicester and had it typed (with significant omissions) and entitled *Diary of a Young Assistant Mistress 1878–1885*. Even at seventeen she saw herself as writing for 'imaginary admirers', and there were aspects of her interests and ambitions which were already ebulliently public. She expected to be heard and listened to.

Clara's diary suddenly registers the end of childhood and schooldays. She announces unceremoniously: 'Next Saturday I am going to Leicester; I am not sure whether I shall like it; but I do know I shall like it better than being at home. The Marxes and Miss Oswald are the only people I care for here.' With this ungracious adieu to family and friends, she embarked on her adult life. Her sister Carrie had started to teach, and the experience was not encouraging: 'Her children are demons. They kick & swear & do nothing else but play cards.' The post of assistant mistress at Wyggeston Girls' School will not present problems of quite that sort, but there will be other problems. Clara notes later:

Very shortly after the announcement of the admission of women to degrees Miss Buss sent for me to her room. With a splendid disregard of her previous insistence on the necessity of my entering a training college before entering the teaching profession she told me that she had recommended me for a post in the new Wyggeston Girls' Grammar School to be opened in Whitsun week. I should only have £80 a year to begin with but Miss Ellen Leicester, the headmistress, would give me every facility for preparing myself for the Intermediate Arts examination in July 1879 and the final B.A. in October 1880 [1st BA and 2nd BA in those days]. Masters from the Boys' Grammar School would give me lessons in Greek and applied mathematics and I could manage Latin and English subjects by myself. A little lady who had been spending some time in our classrooms turned out to be Miss Leicester. Interviews followed with my father first and myself afterwards. I went to Burlington House on Saturday, 15th June, saw my name on the alphabetical honours list of matriculation and was just in time to catch the train to Leicester with no refreshment other than a petrified bun at Kentish Town station. My brother Wilfred met me there and gave me the extra five shillings necessary for a first class ticket.

Leicester's Miss Leicester was presumably bending the rules for Clara. If she arrived 'hardly expecting to enjoy myself', she in fact found it 'delightful'. Her pleasure in her work and in her grown-up life were such that she began 'to get quite nervous as to what particular pain I am to suffer. I have almost presentiments that it will come soon and unexpectedly, otherwise I was never so happy in my life before.' Already, a year after starting as a teacher, she has completed her '1st B.A.' in the 'First Division'. She is studying Greek. She enjoys being a pupil as well as a teacher. Besides teaching and studying and discussing critically, but with interest, the sermons she hears, she skates and walks and swims and takes part in amateur dramatics. Miss Buss wrote to her in 1878 to tell her that 'Miss Leicester speaks of "your quiet, firm, altogether teacher-like manner with the girls". I thought you would like to know her good opinion of you.' Two years later she sent Clara a postcard congratulating her on becoming, at twenty, North London Collegiate's first university graduate. By then, she had a wide circle of friends and acquaintances, most of them connected with school or with the Unitarian community she discovered in Leicester.

In the holidays she goes home, which is now in Coleridge Road, Crouch End, sometimes with a friend. The laundry was given up during those years, and the family moved house. Clara mentions theatre and concert visits, a trip to France with her sisters. A plan to study for an MA waxes and wanes with the tides of enjoyment she feels in her life and her studies. Logic and psychology are added to Greek, and she works hard at calculus for a time. There is a sad, cryptic reference to TM (Tussy Marx), with whom there has been some kind of rift, but there are no other mentions of the Marx family. She is working very hard:

> With the work for school, the mathematics I do, and the mental science I ought to do, my time is filled up. This term however we seem to have been out a great deal & my mind shows a power of feeling excitement about nothing which makes me feel most unwilling to work at anything regularly difficult.

At an occasion organised by the Unitarian chapel she meets Sydney Gimson and his friend Alfred Hopps, the son of the minister, whose sermons can be 'deliciously gloomy'. Alfred comes in for some Clara mockery, but Sydney is different:

> I liked him better that night than I had ever done before. He seemed very sensible, a fact that surprised me. Since, I have come to the conclusion that he is even more than that. He knows & has read ever so much more than A.H. [Alfred Hopps] and although I think he is shy he has a good deal of self-respect.

The young men walk her home, though sometimes Sydney does this on his own. His younger brother Ernest is less in evidence, though Clara kept up with him in later life, and she remembers one occasion when 'he summoned up courage to put his arm round my waist & I nerved myself to corresponding deeds of heroism'. Occasionally, Sydney dances with Clara's friend Polly Blackwell. Perhaps Sydney 'is not a downright Unitarian but rather a Secularist', she speculates, and this probably counts in his favour and inspires another admission that she likes him very much, though with a 'sisterly regard'. She is happy, 'drifting along with the current'. She gets a Valentine with a Cupid on it breaking his bow at the sight of a lady graduate, but Sydney is beginning to show a more obvious interest in Polly, and Clara has a dream that Polly is engaged to her brother Harold. Sydney gives her his confessions to read 'on the way home by the light of the lamps', but 'our evening walks are over now', she comments, and 'Ainsi soit il'.

She thinks a lot about religion and God, and discusses both with Sydney, who calls himself an agnostic, as she has yet to do. 'I believe in God,' she writes,

> because the people I admire most do and because some of their best qualities seem founded upon or at any rate coincident with that belief; sometimes when I feel blissfully happy or dreadfully miserable I believe in him myself but I don't feel any real faith or trust.

A lecture by Arnold Toynbee entitled 'Are Radicals Socialists?' draws more enthusiasm for his looks than his argument, which she thought even less of as time went by. Sydney, who had given her a ticket for the lecture, defends Toynbee's genuineness against her strictures, and Clara admits that people think her hard-hearted.

Her impatience with all the sensible sermons she hears increases, though one, in which it is claimed that 'Longfellow was one of us and must be regarded as the poet of rational religion . . . made me feel a thrill of triumph'. There are picnics and rehearsals with the girls at school, impromptu as well as organised parties, when the young people make speeches on subjects like Women's Rights and Love and Matrimony, and they dance, and Sydney sometimes sings, surprisingly well.

There are more frequent allusions to depression, restlessness, when reading is hard and study impossible. Sydney has something to do with this. She still sees him, but he has 'quite dropped off into a properly polite bowing acquaintance'. There are rumours that he is to be engaged to Polly Blackwell. Then, in March 1883:

> I have been indulging in a fit of hysterical crying tonight. I feel so perfectly wretched & miserable & hopeless & worthless & tired. Instead of working for my exam I have been studying Physical Geography. I can't work for the Exam. The worry of school & the feeling of incompetence make me feel miserable. I do wish I could go to Girton or Univ. College or give up teaching or emigrate.

Clara later put a characteristic gloss on this passage: 'Partly to escape from teachers' meetings at school I was presenting myself at the first examination for the diploma in 1883. The literature of educational theorists was responsible for this inspissated gloom.' There may have

been more to it than that. But she was finding teaching
dull and demanding and was starting to wonder whether
it might be possible to earn her living in some other
way. She was becoming resigned about men. One man
she likes 'immensely' has been married for a week and
a half: 'such is life'. She has accepted that Sydney will
marry someone else. There is a hurt, angry moment
when it seems that the Gimson brothers have left the
Collet girls out of plans to put on another play (Carrie
has by now joined Clara at Wyggeston). She faces up to
this and accepts that it may be due to something difficult in her character.

> I shall never have any intimate friends and I know
> that I undoubtedly possess to a remarkable degree
> the faculty of offending nearly everyone. This is
> partly why I have decided to take to study as hard
> as I can, first in order to ensure my always being
> able to hold a good position as a teacher and sec-
> ondly to have something to fall back upon when
> life seems rather dismal. My school work is inter-
> esting and to a certain degree satisfactory, but my
> views on every subject are growing more and more
> unpopularly unorthodox and I doubt very much
> whether I shall be able to teach children much
> longer; what I care about no one wants taught and
> I do not know other subjects well enough to hold
> my own as a first class teacher. I think I am leaving
> off being a girl.

As part of her teaching diploma she must give a demonstration lesson. This – on Robert Walpole and at her old
school – is watched by Miss Buss and other formidable

judges, under the aegis of the College of Preceptors. She passes, but it is a wretched experience, confirming her determination to leave teaching and go for an MA. She expects bad news, presumably the news that Sydney has become engaged.

A visit to the House of Commons during the school holidays is 'very amusing'. 'Gladstone struck me most as looking so clean. Randolph Churchill did not speak but I conceived rather a sneaking affection for that worthless young man' − a worthless young man whose son Winston would one day be her political master at the Board of Trade and whose letter thanking her for her hard work would be carefully kept by her and perhaps treasured. She is scornful of Parliament and national politics.

> It does not seem possible to feel any enthusiasm for any party whatsoever, they all seem untrue and interested. Parliament is the biggest sham imaginable, local government is grand in comparison; perhaps the reason why women have only individual enthusiasms is owing to their extra penetration; perhaps also it is not.

Back in Leicester in May 1884 she records Sydney Gimson's engagement to a Miss Lovibond, but says no more. Then, out of the blue, she writes that 'E.W. asked me to marry him.' Edward Weymouth seems to have been one of her tutors, perhaps for Latin. She refused him twice, but she kept a bewildered and touching letter he wrote her, in which he hoped she might reconsider his proposal, but understood that if, as she had written, it occasioned her 'such pain, such hopeless pain' he would back off and leave her alone. They seem to have argued about women and marriage and John Stuart Mill's views of both, but he tells her that he thinks of her as 'jolly, tenderhearted, sympathetic, lovable, and less proud than myself'. Perhaps her insistence that, as he puts it, 'you will never love me' is because she is still in love with Sydney.

A happy, three-week visit to Newnham College, Cambridge, where she takes classes in logic and psychology, isn't able to stop her thinking about what she calls 'the E.W. affair', which has made her 'miserable and low'. She distracts herself with study. Work, reading, philosophy become interesting again, though her admiration for George Eliot is accompanied by 'depression at the thought of how wanting my life will be in the fullness of living, owing to my inability to care much for anyone but myself'.

By the middle of 1885, when she was coming to the end of her time as a teacher in Leicester, she writes, 'I have been thinking a good deal about E.W. and am beginning to like him but that will only last till I see him.' She is anxious that he may ask her to marry him again when her spirits are low:

> It is just because I often meet men for whom I have a strong attraction that makes me like them in spite of faults, that I feel sure that if in a moment of depression I imagined I liked him because he was worthy of being loved for his virtues and married him I should grow to hate him & perhaps even fall wildly in love with some one else or feel that I really & truly liked a dozen other men better than I did him. It is much better to live an old maid

and get a little honey from the short real friendships I can have with men for whom I really care
myself, than to be bound for life to a man just
because he thinks he cares for me.

By October 1885 Clara was living in College Hall,
Gordon Square, and studying full time for an MA in
political economy at University College. She was supporting herself on her savings from Leicester (her salary
had risen to £160 after seven years' teaching). She meets
Eleanor Marx again. Both Marx parents have died since
they last met, and Tussy is now living with the Dr
Edward Aveling with whom Clara once studied statistics. It is possible that his still being married to someone
else explains Clara's refusal to visit her old friend – possible, but uncharacteristic of the woman who became
the close friend of George Gissing a few years later;
though she could be surprisingly disapproving of the
working-class girls she was later to interview when she
thought their morals were not all that they ought to
be. It seems more likely, however, that Clara is referring
back to the original cause of the rift when she writes
mysteriously:

Today I spoke to Tussy and we made friends; she
asked me to go and see her & I explained why I
could not; she flushed a little but she knew that I
was not blaming her and that I cared for her as
much as ever. She promised that if ever I could
help her she would ask me. I hope she will if she
needs help & that no cowardice of mine will ever
prevent me from giving help when she asks for it
for herself or anyone she cares for.

Clara's religious and political inheritance contributed to her developing sense of her destiny as a woman. Common sense, straightforwardly thought of as male, but also the imperialist and expansionist energies of a male and liberal world, would need to find a place for her as a woman participating in those traditions. This seems to have entailed a proud refusal on her part to dwell on the constraints she experienced (in fact, 'not complaining' belonged for her with other necessary and unheroic 'male' virtues) and a determined concentration on those organisations and outlets which welcomed her. She attended – and occasionally gave – lectures at the South Place Ethical Society, for instance. Her surprisingly long involvement, from 1888 to at least 1906, with the Charity Organisation Society (COS), to whose *Review* she contributed articles and book reviews, may also be partly explained by her willingness to make use of those channels that were hospitable to women writers.

The COS attracted many Unitarian women during the 1870s and 1880s. Most of them abandoned the organisation and its principles sooner than Clara did. Her continuing adherence to an organisation that Beatrice Potter (later Webb) had already, by the late 1880s, characterised as neither seeking the causes of poverty nor having any cure for it is difficult to explain; though paradoxically, given what we know of the twenty-first century's orthodoxies on development and aid and charity, and the new suspicion of centralised state funding and control, Clara's position may have come back into fashion. The COS emphasis on social investigation and on forms of self-help connects with, and could be seen to have grown out of, the kinds of work she did with

Charles Booth, and it even consorts in some respects with aspects of the government policy she was involved in developing at the Board of Trade: the setting up of trade boards and labour exchanges.

Having taken her MA after two happy years spent mostly in the British Museum Reading Room, Clara returned reluctantly to teaching for a little over a year at her old school. By the beginning of 1888, however, she was also working as an investigator for Booth, as was Beatrice Potter, who had not yet married Sidney Webb. In his *Outcast London*, Gareth Stedman Jones explains the origins of Booth's project:

> Booth first became interested in the condition of the poor after a visit to [Samuel] Barnett in Whitechapel in 1878. Unlike Barnett, however, he envisaged his role as a social investigator rather than as a philanthropist or a charity worker. Booth's ideas on poverty were initially very close to those of the COS. Like the leaders of the Society, he considered that the extent of chronic poverty had been wildly exaggerated by agitators and the sensational writers of the popular press. Significantly, Booth finally committed himself to the task of concrete investigation in response to the crisis of February 1886. His decision to embark upon an extensive enquiry was provoked by Hyndman's claim that 25 per cent of the London population lived in conditions of extreme poverty. Booth intended to refute Hyndman's claim for very much the same reasons that the COS had refuted similar claims about the extent of distress in the previous seven years.

The crisis in February 1886 was a riot of unemployed men in central London, violent and serious enough to cause considerable panic among middle-class Londoners and to create a widely held sense that something must be done immediately about poverty in the city. Stedman Jones goes on to describe how Booth's discovery that 35 per cent of the population of Tower Hamlets were in fact almost always in serious need worked to separate him henceforth from the COS, which regarded the dispensing of relief as deliberate pauperisation. Booth could no longer support the society's administering of charity in ways intended to encourage individual independence and self-help before all else, and many people agreed with him. The COS came to seem remote and anachronistic in its approach to the poor and in its reluctance to involve working people themselves in the forms and the delivery of relief. Clara remained on friendly terms with Charles Booth and his wife Mary. Her letters occasionally make it clear that they and Clara had agreed to differ on these issues and on her continuing support of the COS.

Between 1887 and 1901 Clara became an expert interviewer of women workers, mainly within sectors of the clothing industry, and she turned her findings into statistical evidence and descriptive reports. Another report, published as a parliamentary paper in 1899, was on domestic servants. She had by then contributed long chapters on a range of subjects to Booth's project, including one on school provision for girls in London and another on the conditions of women workers across a range of trades, in small factories and workshops or as piece workers at home. Her interviews furnished her with a pretty exact understanding of the skills required to make boxes, collars, ties, brushes, umbrellas, corsets, trousers. While cleverly highlighting individual cases, she sets these against a picture assembled from her gathered statistics on pay and on married status and their relation to infant mortality figures, for instance, and on the impact of drink on generations of a family. Another thread of her chapter is the presence of Jewish employers and employees within the least-known aspects of the East End economy, which she treats quite fairly, it seems to me. She even has a section on ostrich feather curling, and I wonder rather nervously whether she visited the Salamans' East End hat shop, though perhaps it had moved to the West End by then.

Clara's interviewing meant visiting women's homes and workplaces, and though I cannot imagine her striking the women or the employers she interviewed as grandly patrician, she must have seemed to some of them to have come from another planet. She is free with expressions of exasperation and dismay at the impossible situations in which these women worked and brought up their children, and not above blaming the women themselves at times for wastefulness, incompetence, ignorance, and so on. But her reports are wonderfully detailed and vivid, and she was scrupulously sensitive to the differences among the women and their situations – economic, social and individual differences – and to the undeniable usefulness to them of having skills, however poorly rewarded. The strength of her reports lay in their sense of these women's multiple vulnerabilities in the marketplace to husbands, fathers and employers, so long as limited experience and education made them reluctant to take responsibility for what they produced or for what they were paid. There are moments when she can barely contain her rage:

On the whole, the home-workers are the first to point out that as they have their children to attend to and the meals to prepare, and the washing and mending and cleaning to do, they cannot give very long hours to their work. But unskilled working women – shirt makers, match-box makers, trouser makers – do undoubtedly work very long hours when they have others to support. Life to large numbers of married women in the East End is nothing more than procrastination of death. They bear children and bury them. Their minds have been starved and their senses dulled.

These were productive years, on the other hand, for Clara, between 1887 and 1891. In addition to her work for Booth she was publishing pieces in the *Charity Organisation Review,* in the *Wyggeston Girls' Gazette* and by 1891 in the *Economic Journal.*

In March 1892, George Gissing wrote in his diary that a lecture had been 'delivered . . . by a Miss Clara E. Collet M.A. . . . can't make out what the lecture really was – except that she maintained the "healthiness" of my mind'. She also, according to another report, opposed the idea that Gissing was a fatalist and defended his novels for their combination of idealism and realism. Almost a year later Clara wrote to him, asking if she might call. He refused. She sent copies of some of her articles, and then an invitation to him and to his wife Edith. He still refused. Then, on 18 July 1893, Gissing wrote in his diary:

Richmond by arrangement, I called on Miss Collet at 34 Hill St. We at once went out on to the river,

and rowed to Kingston and back. Home by the
8.45 train. Miss Collet younger than I had expected.
She wishes to come and call on E., but I fear.

This was the year when Gissing's eleventh novel, *The
Odd Women*, was published: too early for Clara to have
inspired its account of the lives of educated, unmarried
women, as she is sometimes thought to have done. In
fact, it was the novel of Gissing's she liked least, 'so much
that I nearly did not make George Gissing's acquaintance because of it'. Gissing was thirty-six when he met
Clara, three years older than she was. He was married
for the second time, to a 'respectable working-class' girl
he had picked up in Camden Town three years earlier.
At this point there was one child, Walter.

Almost as soon as they met, Gissing confided in Clara
both his despair at his current marriage and, soon after,
the dark and guilty secret of his youth. As a poor scholarship student at Owens College in Manchester he had
stolen small amounts of money in order to support an
alcoholic young prostitute called Nell with whom he
had become obsessed. The college expelled him. After
a year's exile in America, where he survived by selling
stories to newspapers and magazines, he returned and
married Nell. The marriage was a nightmare for them
both. As she drank herself to death, Gissing paid fifteen
shillings a week for her to board in a Battersea nursing
home until she died there in 1888.

Clara, as his friend, became bizarrely implicated in
Gissing's living-out of a dilemma which must have been
entirely alien to her, though it was one with which she
seems to have been determined to sympathise. His
snobbery and fastidiousness, and his feelings of social

inferiority, made him seek out as sexual partners women he regarded as *his* social inferiors. Yet his dream of a life's partner who would share his intellectual interests while gracing his home remained unfulfillable, given his sense of his sexual nature as both importunate and squalid. The lines of his friendship with Clara were set early on, and by him. He told her about his domestic trials and his sexual history. His announcement that his wife is pregnant again arrives in the midst of a spate of letters complaining about her sluttishness, shrewishness and stupidity. Alongside these confessions go congratulations to Miss Collet on her intelligence and strength, her good sense, good fortune and good health. He thanks her for her kindness, and within a few months of their meeting she has offered to pay for Walter's schooling and has taken Edith on an outing. Gissing reassures Clara that his wife 'does not now misinterpret your position'. Less than a year later he writes to her:

> A strange thing that, but for our having come to know each other, these struggles & gaspings of mine would have been unspoken of to anyone. I suppose my reason for telling you of such miseries is the assurance I have that you cannot be depressed by them; you are the sole & single person of my acquaintance who is living a healthy, active life, of large intercourse with men and women . . . You are unassociated & unassociable with gloom.

Edith does not misinterpret Clara's position because Gissing has rendered his new friend untroubling and untroubled, a person removed from and immune to sexual feeling and its dangerous consequences.

Clara gets him to read Maria Edgeworth and a life of Adam Smith and reproves him for affectations of style. He is 'always glad when you feel able to praise my writing'; less glad when she rebukes him for unkindness or impatience towards his wife and child. Many of his complaints are about the impossibility of inviting friends home. He is ashamed of his wife and of the acrimony and chaos of his household. Clara seems to have taken this in her stride and simply insisted on visiting him.

By 1897 things had come to a head. Gissing left his wife, sending his son Walter to live with his family in Wakefield, while the baby, Alfred, stayed with his mother. For a few months Gissing and Clara expressed more of their feelings for one another in their letters, and there was a fevered one to her from Rome in January 1898. He is ill and unhappy.

> We are now pretty old friends, & yet I find that I am only just beginning really to know you. I have always inclined to think of you as very self-reliant, rather scornful of weaker people & especially impatient of anything like sentimental troubles. There is no harm in saying that your last two or three letters have pleased me just because they differed in some respects from those of a year or two ago. I used to feel that, however friendly, you regarded me with a good deal of disapprobation & perhaps a little lurking contempt. Well, I know that a certain amount of contempt you must feel for me, & always will; but you are gentler than of old. And rightly so. One who suffers incessantly – even though as the result of his own folly – should not be sternly treated.

The letter slides, typically, into a rehearsal of his woes, ailments and deserts, and a rejection of her offer to come and look after him should he need her to. He makes her his executor and begs her to use her 'strong brain and pure woman's heart to guard my boys against the accursed temptations of early life'. Since Clara then noted that Gissing met Gabrielle Fleury on 10 February 1898, and that she, Clara, destroyed Gissing's letters to her between that date and 22 July 1899, there must be some connection between the two events. She also notes without comment that Gissing had written to her of Gabrielle as 'a French woman of the finest type and infinitely graceful', and writes that 'my letters to G.G. were much more formal from this time forward'.

It seems likely that Clara made some kind of declaration to Gissing after his separation from Edith, which he elaborately (and perhaps even tactfully) turned down. Among Clara's papers is a story called 'Undercurrents', written in her handwriting and signed Clover King. Its plot, characters and theme suggest that Clara drew on her knowledge of Gissing's early life, as well as on her own inadmissible feelings for him, to write it. It is a romance between a professional woman and a brilliant scientist with a murky past. The heroine is Marian, a woman in her late twenties, who enjoys considerable freedom, knows men, does men's work and is happy. She is, however, charged by some of her women friends with being 'a time-server and a trimmer', because she defends the decision of one of them, a doctor, to marry a stockbroker. Staying with Marian is a young teacher called Maggie, who is pretty, while Marian has 'no looks to speak of'. They are together when they meet Frank Rust, a scientific 'genius' and a contemporary of Maggie's from Cambridge. The older Marian instantly distrusts him, while Maggie encourages his interest in herself. But when he proposes to her, hinting at something disgraceful in his past, Maggie is overcome by revulsion. Marian still distrusts him, but is touched by his lack of belief in himself as someone who might at all plausibly be loved.

Two years later and the two women are at Frank's 'brilliant' lecture, when it is interrupted by a girl drunkenly shouting, 'That's my 'usband, that is. My! Aint he a toff. Three cheers for Frankie.' Frank shamefully disowns her, but resigns his post at University College as well.

Marian is moved to help Frank and discovers that his wife Mollie is terminally ill with a hereditary disease as well as being pregnant and an alcoholic. Marian grows fond of her, especially for so unswervingly loving her husband. Meanwhile, Maggie marries a dull barrister, amusingly encountered on the Metropolitan Line in a scene which might have provided a rare comic moment in a Gissing novel. Mollie dies, and before long Marian's deep-blue eyes are startling Frank with their unexpected lights. After a solemn kiss, likened to a sacrament, and some difficulties as they try to come clean about what they feel, Frank and Marian decide to marry. 'It is no sacrifice,' said Marian, with glowing eyes, 'I love you.'

This is not a very successful short story. It is significant, though, that Clara, scourge of sentimentality, found this an appropriate form for expressing some of the facts and feelings of her friendship with Gissing and her secret hopes for it. Perhaps there were no other models for such a story or even such a relationship, and telling it as a romance made it to some extent both recognisable and containable, by putting it firmly and ironically in its place as no more than a daydream. Several lesbian novels have used the conventions of the romance in rather similar ways, as if those conventions might be faithful to women's experience of sexual desire by virtue of signalling their difference from traditional male accounts. Male sexuality is a central concern for all the women characters in the story, and Frank's sexuality, aberrant and hard to accommodate as it is, is offered as a finer thing than Maggie's barrister's could ever be. Marian's settling for a difficult and uncomfortable marriage is accorded a sort of heroism. Sacrificing her hard-won power and independence for this offer of male sexuality is seen as simultaneously dangerous and promising.

Marian's dilemma – and it may have been Clara's – is that she wants to possess male genius and male sexuality, doubly: for themselves and for herself. Marian's identification with Frank is with the unlovable, the delinquent man. His shame matches her reticence and his awkwardness her sexual inexperience. The romance form works to express female desire for male power as well as male love, and a pleasure in fantasies of capitulation to both.

Gabrielle Fleury began living with Gissing in 1899. Her family insisted on a pseudo-wedding ceremony, but they were never married. Gabrielle called herself Madame Gissing to the day she died and was always uncomfortable with the irregularity of their union, for which she never quite forgave Gissing. Earlier that year he wrote to Gabrielle:

> A day or two ago I wrote to Miss Collet, telling her how glad I should be if any way could be found for a legitimate marriage, but that I feared. – To-day she replies: 'Can you not impress upon Gabrielle that, here in England, the best men and women recognize love and loyalty and courage?'

Clara had reminded him about George Eliot and George Lewes.

When Gissing died in 1903, Gabrielle and he had spent four years together, often in France with her mother (whom he disliked and accused of starving him). They were, in fact, four years punctuated by long and bitter separations. Clara was kept informed of the pleasures and pains of it all by Gissing and, before long, by Gabrielle too. Since Clara was the executor, with Gissing's brother, of a will which left what little there was to Edith and her sons, and nothing to Gabrielle, communication between the two women became necessary. They met, on the first anniversary of Gissing's death, in St Jean-de-Luz, where he had died. When Gabrielle left after a visit to England later that summer, Clara wrote (somewhat surprisingly) in her diary: 'I miss her more than I have missed anyone.'

She came to assume almost total responsibility for Gissing's affairs, his books as well as his family. She struggled to agree plans with H. G. Wells to reissue Gissing's out-of-print novels and encouraged a mooted biography by Morley Roberts, a dodgy old friend of Gissing's and eventual author of *The Private Life of Henry Maitland* – by then a novel rather than a 'life' – which earned him Clara's disapproval, though they remained friends. Indeed, their correspondence during 1904 and 1905, when he was beginning to think about a book on Gissing, contains interesting discussions by her of Gissing's and Roberts's novels, though she also hedges her bets with the line, 'I have occasional flashes of humility which would always prevent my attempting any critical estimate of George's work.' Her letters to Roberts are not only affectionate, they are revealing about her life and her sense of herself. Only very occasionally, she admits, does she feel that she is doing a valuable job at the Board of Trade. 'For months at a time I speculate whether it is honest to go on drawing a salary at public expense for such poor results.' She also sets her own investigative work alongside his and Gissing's work as novelists: 'I take your experience as you give it in *Immortal Youth* seriously, and I am giving you mine because from the very nature of things, our experience is mutually exclusive and you may be glad to imagine it. You as a novelist and I as an investigator of things concerning women are bound to know and to think as rightly as we can.' Wells eventually backed off as a trustee, exasperated by Clara as much as by the Gissing family and Gabrielle. Clara negotiated reissues on her own, even of her least favourite, *The Odd Women*, and she appears single-handedly to have arranged with 10 Downing Street for a Civil List pension to be granted to Gissing's sons 'in recognition of the literary services of their father and of his straitened circumstances'.

Gabrielle, meanwhile, took over many of Gissing's dependent habits in her friendship with Clara. She wrote to her regularly and plangently, on a restricted number of obsessive topics. Her health was of a kind to require the attention of 'my doctors' rather than a doctor; and these were always unanimously and obligingly ready to forbid her doing things she didn't want to do: travel, move flats, see people, attend to their needs. Clara was expected to confirm the wisdom of this choral advice. Like many an evolved hypochondriac, Gabrielle lived to a great age. I was introduced to her as she sat bolt upright in her Paris apartment in the late 1940s, and I had been firmly reminded to address her clearly and often as Madame Gissing. Clara loved her and was entirely loyal to her, though their friendship cooled with time. It was probably not until about 1914 that she received a letter from Gabrielle that was neither self-absorbed nor hectoring.

You can detect in Clara's diaries of the years up to the First World War a confidence and pleasure in life not

always apparent before that. She knows herself to be trusted, relied on, immensely capable and knowledgeable. She is asked for her advice on the education of daughters and other matters and she trusts her own instincts. She became friendly during these years with the French writer Romain Rolland and his sister Madeleine; and this was the period when, above all, she consolidated friendships of all kinds, while admitting humorously that her occasional swoops on her family were dreaded for – as she put it herself – her 'masterfulness' and 'tactlessness and general overbearingness'.

She carried on an impressive correspondence. During the early years of the twentieth century, for instance, she was communicating with the Cambridge economists Herbert Foxwell (who had been her tutor at University College London), Alfred Marshall and Maynard Keynes

about the curriculum of the Economics Tripos there and
of the degree course being set up at the London School
of Economics, in the interests of developing Economics
as an academic discipline which would prepare 'men' for
business as well as the academy. She weathered or avoided
the bad relations sourly circulating among these academics, and their warring politics. She became friendly,
and kept up a long correspondence, with several
American women working in fields close to her own.
Edith Abbott, for instance, was an academic from
Nebraska, who became a dean at Chicago University.
Her life's work and her interests – the academic investigation of poverty, particularly as it affected women
through drunkenness or widowhood, but also the collecting of evidence about dockers and cotton workers
– were something like an American version of Clara's
work for Booth's London investigation.

Her work changed in 1909. This meant attending
meetings in the office of Winston Churchill, the
President of the Board of Trade, with a group of politicians, civil servants and invited advisers, including Sidney
Webb and William Beveridge, who were working at
speed to draft a new Trade Boards Bill. Clara had experience of giving evidence to the Select Committee on
'Home Work' and was there to contribute what she knew
about women workers generally. She writes about
Churchill:

I don't think the Board of Trade loves Mr Churchill;
but I confess that he interests me as a human being
whatever his faults may be. It is partly because I
only know 'intellectuals' or 'thoughtful men' that
this type of person governing them appeals to a

side of me which might belong to a respectable Bohemian.

Lord Robert Cecil appeals to her even more. He 'is like a gentle highly intelligent monk'. She notices how the men treat her:

Mr Churchill 'damned that fellow C . . .' and then apologised to me for doing so. It is very amusing to contrast the different ways in which they treat me. Mr A . . . [a colleague she disliked] aims at treating me like a man with no more respect than a man in the same place; all the others treat me with a little more consideration because I am a woman, but quite rightly don't put themselves out for me, and treat me as a colleague.

Clara's contribution to the discussions she describes covered a vast range of women's employment – especially work done by married women at home. This was still, of all categories of work, the least susceptible to minimum wage regulation and most likely to be performed by women in desperate straits. It still is.

Clara's initial pleasure at working with politicians rapidly turned to an impatience that was to explode in 1910 with her abortive resignation, which fills many pages of her diary. Afterwards, she records decorous conversations about it all with the knighted and other gentlemen with whom she worked. Yet her exasperation is finally with them, the very men who confer on her such power and influence as she would ever have. And while this is going on, 'very important questions come up', which need someone of her experience to deal with them. She is 'having a good many qualms of conscience'. There are questions too about her own life, her estimate of her work and achievements, her pension, who might be appointed in her place.

Then the crisis is over and she agrees to stay. But she is fifty and it is time to think about the future, money, retirement, perhaps a cottage in the country. The incident stands for the anomalous predicament of professional women at a time when no woman might vote or stand for Parliament, or be married in the Civil Service before 1937, and when women's 'expertise' was understood to emerge from their natures and to be expendable.

Clara published *Educated Working Women*, a book of essays, in 1902, and dedicated it to the memory of Miss Buss. She starts with the differences between 'the great majority of women, [who] belong to the working classes and spend their youth as wage-earners, in many cases under conditions injurious to mind and body, although the real work of their lives is eventually to be found in their own homes', and middle-class women, many of whom will need to become self-supporting, since the imbalance between men and women in the middle classes is such that 'to expect a hundred women to devote their energies to attracting fifty men seems slightly ridiculous'. She delicately picks out the contradictions inherent in the refusal of the ancient universities to admit women to degrees, even as they maintain that women are by nature incapable of studying to this level: 'The futility of forbidding women to do what they were incapable of doing was never perceived by the opponents of the movement for the higher education of women, who based their opposition on this ground.' She also goes on to write that 'it is now at least admitted that the rather-above-the-average woman is quite on a level with the average man', without spelling out the historical and cultural assumptions underlying such a proposition.

Clara accepted many of the nature/culture oppositions of her day, because she had lived them. She did believe that women differed from men in their 'nervous organisation' and in their 'emotional nature', though she believed in the power of education and literature to reinforce prejudice and to undermine it. She wrote in a letter to Morley Roberts in 1904, for instance, 'I used to have so little confidence in my own feelings that I have always been a little nervous about professing friendship for anyone.' She believed 'that women come to intellectual maturity later than men', and though she attributed this to their 'nature' she was scathing about the uses to which such a 'truth' might be put. She writes of teachers: 'Their youth and inexperience are facts constantly brought before them up to the age of thirty or thereabouts, and then with hardly an interval they find themselves confronted by this theory of sudden decay of faculties in women.'

In her own life, Clara struggled to ensure her prospects in a world which might well be expected to find her wanting in 'femininity', though she also saw 'femininity' as a condition of human weakness, which bizarrely attracted to itself the valuable reward of supportive and even occasionally stimulating male company. She criticised the 'excessive femininity' of *Women and Economics* by the writer Charlotte Perkins Gilman, writing under her married name of Mrs Stetson, though she applauded and agreed with the American writer's insistence that 'women are growing honester, braver, stronger, more healthful and skilful and able and free – more human in all ways', so long as such improvements were seen to be the consequence of women's greater economic independence. But human strengths were for Clara, by and large, male strengths, to be sought by women as by men. She did not call herself a feminist and came to think of herself as a suffragist but not a suffragette. Yet a central and compelling theme of her life was women and how they lived and worked and managed their lives in marriages or on their own.

By 1910 the campaign for women's suffrage had exploded into occasional violence. There were demonstrations, arson attacks and picture-slashing. My Jewish step-grandmother chained herself and her sisters to the railings of Holborn Post Office, and they were carried off to jail. Their family was richer than the Collets, and though the girls were brought up to have accomplishments and intellectual interests they were neither educated nor trained to earn their living. Clara lived by her own labours. She voted for the Liberal Party until almost the end of her life, when she voted (as my Jewish grandfather did just after the Second World War) for the Labour Party. She never thought of herself as a socialist, and despite her childhood friendship with the Marx family appears not to have read very much by Marx in either German or English and apparently thought him 'uninteresting' as an economist. Her formation was liberal, Unitarian and utilitarian, rationalist and reformist – traditions which were neither more nor less hospitable to efforts to improve women's lives than many socialist ones. She would have shied away from the least hint of Utopianism.

Clara's sometimes adjuring voice is an odd one. Her

speech, in fact, seemed to waver in pitch in her old age, and she spoke with a slight lisp. The voice to be heard in her writing is sometimes scornful, sarcastic, but it can also be modest and proud. She lived out clusters of contradictions in her education, her work and her private life, and the beliefs and values to which she was loyal sometimes required her to denigrate aspects of herself and her sex in order to function effectively. What marks her out from many of her contemporaries (though not altogether from mine) is that her working life, which took part in these contradictions, required her to collect and describe facts and figures about other women's experiences, particularly working-class women's experiences. This meant mastering a language and discipline of distance, impersonality, authority, which helped to shape the ways in which women's experiences of the kind she was researching might be discussed and treated thereafter. She was expected to sympathise in an especially womanly way *and* to disengage from those she investigated. Social investigation of the sort she and other women pioneered was to be seen as appropriate work for women – and therefore potentially suspect. The anomalies of her position as a worker, vis-à-vis male authority and female experience, also affected her own life and its more public privacies. None of her relations with other people were quite of a kind to fit the stories that could be told about them.

Taxes on Knowledge

My mother was right: Clara wasn't as nice as her sisters, and she knew she wasn't. She sometimes confessed to cold-heartedness, though not to beadiness, to worldliness or to the ambition that took her into a career that veered subtly away from her father's campaigning spirit and gentle, lifelong rebelliousness. Yet it was she who turned herself into her family's historian, tracking the family name back to the Middle Ages, transcribing and privately publishing sets of letters written by her ancestors and close relations from the early eighteenth century onwards, assembling more than two centuries of papers as an archive; hoping and planning, presumably, to write and publish the family's history, though never quite getting to the point of saying what she thought of them all: the colonial adventurers or the excitable early Dissenters, her intellectual aunt and great-aunt; or her busy, practical and finally disgruntled mother, or even Eliza, her paternal grandmother, the recipient of dozens of dourly wooing letters from the cousin she eventually married – letters which Clara collected and turned into a book much later on. I recognise a double impulse in her: to escape her family, to live separately from them, but also to make reparation to them for doing so, to apologise for the impatience she so often felt, especially in her childhood and adolescence, with what she must sometimes have thought of as their ineffectual decency, their virtue, their Utopianism – her father's especially. Perhaps I do more than recognise her motives in all this. I identify with them, and I have ransacked her archive. This chapter depends on Clara and the history she began to put together. The lives she wanted to record and remember were ones I could only know through her and from what my father learned from her and told me.

In 1891 a story of Clara's was published in a magazine called *Home Chimes*, in which a pretty young teacher, icily independent, condescends to preside at the deathbed of a miserable young man who has fallen in love with her from his lodgings across the road. She returns to her room at the end of the story, where she 'threw herself on the bed and wept bitterly, not because Mark Hailstone was dead, but because Mark Hailstone's death was nothing to her'.

Clara's stories and diaries make it clear that she believed physical as well as mental and emotional toughness were absolute requirements for any young woman who meant to have interesting and rewarding work and to live alone. But she sometimes dwelled on her restlessness and on moments of depression and even despair, as she contemplated what she must therefore do without and turn herself into. Another of her heroines recognises 'emotional solitude' as a condition she shares with certain men as well as women. Clara learned in her family to think of herself as hard-hearted and unlovable. She did much better in her grown-up life with friends and colleagues, yet she was always drawn back to the family that told her what was wrong with her, forced her to acknowledge her insensitivity, her obstinacy, her selfishness. Her brother Harold, for instance, must have felt he

had her measure when he wrote to their great-aunt
Mary about his twenty-four-year-old younger sister:

> I did not think of Clara going to Newnham when
> I last wrote to you. I do not think she had then
> formed the idea. But I felt that she is not likely to
> remain long content with the same position, no
> matter how pleasant or safe. I fancy she has the
> intention of going to the Bar if women are ever
> admitted; her private studies are all more or less in
> that direction. She is not likely to confess to such
> a desire for fear of ridicule. Meantime she looks
> forward to being Head Mistress of a good public
> school, but even there she will not rest unless she
> has everything her own way. She is very self-reliant,
> but not objectionably so.

His final comment was prompted, I suspect, by a sense
of his great-aunt's high-minded expectations when it
came to putting a woman's intelligence to the service
of others, as she had done as a teacher of girls all her
life. Mary appears to have sailed triumphantly into her
nineties on a conviction that good sense in religion as
in life was what made the world go round.

In *Culture and Anarchy*, Matthew Arnold asks where
the philistinism and the 'undeniable provincialism' of
Protestant Nonconformists come from, and concludes
that 'the Nonconformist is not in contact with the main
current of national life'. Arnold may not have been
thinking of Unitarians when he delivered his diatribe,
but Clara would have recognised her family in some of
it. And Harold was right about Clara's ambitions. Both
she and their brother Wilfred were to occupy positions

in the world their father had in some ways cocked a snook at: Clara at the Board of Trade and Wilfred in the Colonial Service. Clara herself had not only to overcome the disadvantages of being a woman in the process, she also had to come to terms with her own sometimes uncomfortable membership of a group, and a particular family, for whom protest and political campaigns conducted from the margins and against the government and other powerful interests were quite simply the stuff of life.

Her father was born in 1813 and named Collet by his parents, John and Eliza Dobson, who were first cousins. Collet was the maiden name of both their mothers, of their shared grandparents, and it was the name of those of his ancestors he knew most about, so that not long after his father's death, he added another (unhyphenated) Collet to the end of his name, to become Collet Dobson Collet. This may also have been to distinguish himself from his Dobson siblings, three at least of whom transported themselves to New Zealand or Australia in the late 1830s, where they joined the Established Church (one at least as a clergyman), perhaps for lack of a Unitarian chapel or congregation in the places to which they migrated. He may also have wanted to commemorate his mother's favourite brother, Captain Collet Barker, who has been described as 'a veteran of Napoleonic campaigns and humane friend to Aboriginal people', who was, nonetheless, killed 'by unfamiliar Aborigines who mistook him for a rapacious sealer' in 1831. He was consulted about his nephew's future before going to Australia and afterwards. Collet's younger sister Sophia became a Dobson Collet too, explaining that 'in everything public I am ever likely to do, I should like to be known as Collet's sister'. I shall return to Sophy and her surprisingly public life and to her parents.

Collet was sent to Bruce Castle School in Tottenham, a 'progressive' school of the time, founded in 1817 by Rowland Hill, later the inventor of penny postage, who made the school famous for its faith in self-discipline rather than punishment, its religious agnosticism and its reliance on 'voluntary' virtue rather than competition. Dickens admired the school's methods as 'the only recognition of education as a broad system of moral and intellectual philosophy that I have ever seen in practice'. A sort of Regency Bedales. Collet appears to have enjoyed himself there and to have edited the first of his many magazines while at school, though he suffered from a depressive illness when he was fourteen or so, at the time of his father's death at forty-nine. The school reported this episode to his mother in some detail, assuring her that her son's recovery was now imminent, perhaps as a result of the hope 'expressed by his father in his last moments that he would qualify himself to be the instructor and protector of his mother and sisters'.

Collet went on to University College London in 1832 to study law as one of that institution's earliest student cohorts. Hale Bellot's 1929 history of the college includes a memory of Collet and his brother Charles there in 1833, editing a student magazine called *The London University Examiner*, which was circulated in manuscript.

It made it its special business to report the proceedings of student societies. The first number was issued on the 22nd of January, 1833. The magazine came to an end with the fifteenth number issued on the 22nd May, having reached some five hundred pages. It was a very vigorous and radical journal, containing articles on Irish misrule, the Ministry, of which it was very critical, the discussion of political questions in literary and scientific institutions, national education, church reform, slavery, and the rights of women, with reports of the proceedings of the National Political Union, and an indignant protest against the way in which the authorities handled the meeting in Cold Bath Fields.

For two years after finishing at University College, Collet worked as an attorney's clerk in Gray's Inn, before deciding to leave the law and train as a singer. He was well into his twenties by then, the oldest son in a family of seven children (an older sister became an Anglican nun), and there must have been financial worries about his widowed mother and his much younger sister, Sophy, since he was called upon by a cousin to justify his decision, though he did so with no sense of having anything much to apologise for. He had been helped by his great-aunt Anne to pay for his three years of musical training (working at the piano as well as his singing), and he was certain that by teaching and lecturing as well as performing he would ultimately be able to make a reasonable living. Besides, he insisted, music had other advantages over the law:

> The promotion of harmony is surely as respectable at the least as the management of discord. And if society in its progress towards perfection should dispense with one of the two professions, she will certainly get rid of the lawyers.

He had maintained and developed his political interests during these years, and by 1841 he was involved with various Chartist groups, including the Anti-Corn-Law League and the People's Charter Union, which was to evolve into the Association for the Repeal of the Taxes on Knowledge (and which campaigned to get the stamp duty on newspapers removed). He spent most of 1840 acting in repertory in Leeds, living in theatrical digs; and his mother, who wrote constantly and anxiously to him throughout that year, conspired with him in his brief incarnation as Julian Collet, actor. The acting faded out, however, and during the rest of the 1840s and the early years of the 1850s he survived by singing and lecturing (sometimes combining the two, as when he gave a series of illustrated lectures on music in Shakespeare's plays).

And all this time he was writing articles. These were mostly about the stamp duty and its implications for the education and political understanding of working people and for the dissemination of critical and radical opinions generally, but also about a whole range of political issues at home and abroad. He identified himself all his life as a Teacher of Singing, and his children remembered him principally as singing in the chorus at Covent Garden. It is clear, though, that as time went by his entirely unremunerated work for the repeal of the stamp duty on daily and weekly newspapers took up most of his time and energies. Later, after the campaign had succeeded, that work led to his spending most of his time editing magazines and organising local 'working men's foreign affairs' pressure groups, and at the end of his life running another campaign, this time against the tax levied on small railway companies and passed on to passengers: a tax which he believed impinged unfairly on

great numbers of poor and relatively poor workers. He
could be described as a 'single issue' man, politically, if
serially so, but his causes were well chosen and they
came out of and contributed to a radical politics. He
wrote at the end of his life:

> Our movement for the repeal of the Stamp was a
> political movement in every sense of that ill under-
> stood word. We claimed the repeal as a right. We
> detested the Stamp Duty not because it was a tax
> on those who paid, but because it was a prohibi-
> tion on those who could not pay it. And it was to
> write and print for ourselves that we claimed; not
> merely to read what other people might be so good
> as to write and print for us.

As secretary of the Association for the Repeal of the
Taxes on Knowledge in the 1840s and early 1850s, he
wrote articles and letters to the press and hundreds of
letters to famous and influential men of his day. He got
replies from a good many of them: Carlyle supported
the cause, for instance, but wanted nothing to do with
the campaign; Leigh Hunt had lost Collet's original letter,
but if another were sent he could guarantee attendance
at a meeting, and so on. Clara preserved these letters
along with the family ones, though their signatures are
their only value or interest in most cases. She remembered being paid 6d a week by her father for pasting
some of the useful ones into a 'guard' or loose-leaf book.
There are friendly, non-committal letters from Dickens
and Wilkie Collins, some much more interested ones
from John Stuart Mill, and others from Lord Stanley in
the House of Lords and Charles Dilke in the House of

Commons. Gladstone wrote from 11 Downing Street to ask exactly how the taxes on paper worked out in relation to other taxes on wood products and what would be lost to the Treasury if they were removed. Richard Cobden became a member of the committee and an active, friendly colleague, inclined to tease Collet about the curious mélange of music and logic that characterised the fund-raising and publicity events he organised. 'You are a very cool young gentleman!' he remarked admiringly in one letter. Collet's old friend, the music publisher Vincent Novello, helped him out with the music on at least one occasion. There was long and detailed correspondence with several of the other men who worked with him on the campaign: Francis Place, John Bright, George Lewes, Thomas Milner-Gibson, who is credited with getting the final Bill through the House of Commons.

When Collet died in 1898, an obituary in the *Daily News* reminded readers that an earlier generation of editors had simply defied the laws on stamp duty and gone to prison or paid the swingeing fines, in the hope of drawing public attention to the absurdity of the law. Or they had reacted rather as Coleridge had fifty years earlier: bringing out his pro-Unitarian weekly *Watchman* in 1796 on every eighth day in order to avoid the stamp tax. 'Mr Collet's tactics,' his obituarist pointed out, 'were of a milder but more effective kind' than most. Indeed, they were to bear fruit in 1855, when the stamp duty on newspapers was eventually abolished, though the taxes on paper were not repealed until 1861.

In the early 1850s, Collet toured the North of England in order to drum up support for his campaign and meet the editors and owners of local papers and magazines to discuss particular cases and tactics. He went to Dunfermline in Scotland in 1853, where he met Jane Marshall, a young widow with a printing shop, a sort of newsagent's, it seems, in which she sold penknives and other oddments and ran a small lending library. She also edited, printed and sold the local *Dunfermline News*; and she appears to have thought up a strategy for avoiding the tax due on her fortnightly paper by calling alternate issues of it the *Dunfermline Register*. Forty years later, when he was in his eighties and writing what became a two-volume account of this campaign, called *History of the Taxes on Knowledge: Their Origin and Repeal*, Collet recalled how they had backed and made use of Jane's canny example – and others – in order to test and demonstrate the unfairness, irrationality, unevenness and slipperiness of the law. He also wrote about the value of this particular local paper and why papers like it should be exempt from tax. 'It really supplied a want,' he wrote, 'that of a means by which people living in the same town might communicate their thoughts to each other, about their civic affairs, their common institutions and their differences in religion, politics, manners and art.' In addition, he praised her twin papers for their use of Scottish dialect alongside a more literary version of English and for their 'liberty of spelling'.

Collet wrote to Jane Marshall, and she wrote back, taking very few liberties of spelling, at first about her scheme for avoiding stamp duty and then about the articles (a parliamentary review and one on the government's foreign policy) she wanted him to write for her paper. By the middle of 1854 he had proposed marriage to her and been accepted. There were complications. She had to dispose of her business, sell the stock, find someone to take over her shop. She wondered whether she should bring her feather bed with her. There was her son Tom to think about and her family, one member of which pressed upon her the possibility that she was about to marry 'a scheming blackguard'. She knew that if Collet was hardly that, he was certainly in no position to support a family in much style; so that even before she had married and left Scotland she had decided she would need to have a business in London and that it might as well be a laundry. In her reply to Aunt Mary's welcoming letter, praising her nephew – 'you could not find one more upright and pure hearted than he is or with a more kind and generous disposition' – Jane wrote:

It must not be expected that with my utmost anxiety to conform to the manners and habits of those

I must come in hourly contact with, I can at once throw aside those I have derived from my infancy from a country and pursuits in which our manners, habits and prejudices are as different as are my idiom or accent from those of your country, but I will take instruction without offence.

Collet and Jane (or Jean, as he called her) were married at the end of 1854. They lived for a year or two in his rooms off the Gray's Inn Road, which doubled as his office. By the time they moved into Sunny Bank and the laundry Jane ran from there for about twenty years, they must have had at least two children. Jane's business card sets the laundry (and their home) in an

improbable 'acre and a half, surrounded by fields. No houses near. Between Highgate Archway and Hornsey Rise.' The land had been a market garden, and still contained beautiful fruit trees, while the house had a 'singing room' and 'no drawing room and no nursery, but a fair sized landing opening into surrounding rooms'. Jane and Collet produced five children altogether in seven years, and her handsome son Tom adopted the name Collet, and Collet himself as his father, and became a much loved brother to them all, eventually going into interesting, if rather unsuccessful, business ventures with Harold (their third child and second son), most of them to do with the practical application of new technologies. They had early and, it seems, hazardous dealings with the beginnings of domestic electricity and with water softening, which may have been useful to their mother's laundry. Indeed, Harold later wrote a book on water softening and purification which was published – to somewhat minimal acclaim, I imagine, though it went into a revised second edition. Tom died young, and there was a lingering sense in the family that Harold never got over his loss or regained his business confidence.

Once the newspaper tax campaign had ended in 1855, Collet became the printer, the publisher and, for most of the time, the editor and a principal contributor, of a series of periodicals – chiefly the *Free Press* – all in some way developed and kept going as vehicles for the ideas of David Urquhart, an eccentric one-time Tory MP and later diplomat, who had been recalled from Constantinople in 1837 because of his openly expressed hostility to Russia. Urquhart and his followers – and clearly Collet was one of them for a time – were bent above all on attacking Lord Palmerston's foreign policy, especially in relation to what they saw as Britain's collusion with Russia's Tsarist regime to destabilise the Ottoman Empire. Lajos Kossuth and Giuseppe Mazzini, who were political refugees in London during the 1850s, were among those somewhat wildly fingered by Urquhart as Russian agents. Mazzini, who wrote a letter remonstrating with the *Free Press* about this, later became a friend of Collet's sister, Sophy, and a note he wrote, presumably to Collet, suggests that a letter from Sophy 'is fully repaying me for all this foolish slander coming from Mr Urquhart and Co.'. Clara remembered that her father entertained a 'lasting regret' for his support of Urquhart, though, 'every one else forgave him'. She also recalled the time when her father was publishing the journal. It had meant, she believed, his 'accepting (and to some extent desiring) prosecution for any libellous matter contained in the *Review*'.

Between 1856 and 1877, when Urquhart died, and funding for the paper presumably ceased (a Mr Isaac Ironside seems to have paid the bills), this protean publication was gradually transformed from a four-page weekly broadsheet newspaper called the *Free Press,* and based in Sheffield, to a monthly magazine the size of the *New Statesman,* published in London and called the *Diplomatic Review,* and finally to a quarterly journal by the same name, but half the size. The scope of the journal's subject matter and opinions shrank, too, over these years: there was more and more of Urquhart and less and less of anyone else. From the beginning the *Free Press* was presented as having no party allegiances. Its surprising claims for itself were that 'it addresses a nation which has forgotten the Law', and 'ignores public opinion and addresses itself to individual judgement'.

Collet's long friendship with Karl Marx may have started during his campaigning days, but it was consolidated in 1856 with the publication of a piece from Marx in the *Free Press* on the fall of Kars and the conduct of the Crimean War, and from July of that year with the serialisation, over nine or ten issues of the *Free Press* and then the *Diplomatic Review*, of the first three chapters of Marx's *Revelations of the Diplomatic History of the Eighteenth Century*, which regularly occupied about a quarter of the paper. During the period of their publication a mysterious F. Marx wrote regularly to the paper, and once or twice later to Collet himself, to remonstrate mildly with his namesake, whose books and articles he clearly read, though he wrote that *Das Kapital* was 'unreadable, much of it, except to someone who has an object in reading it. The abuses under the Factory system will no doubt be read, and that is the only part of the book wh. can be popularly read.' His letters came from Alresford in Hampshire rather than Cheshire, but it is tempting to wonder whether this was the disguised and watchful Engels keeping an eye on Marx and his journalistic flights, pieces of which Engels famously disapproved, but which on numerous occasions he actually wrote himself (in ghostly fashion) or co-wrote. Perhaps – and it's a good deal more likely – this was the Captain Marx who started the fire brigade in Alresford in 1879, a man who may have become easily inflamed by anything incendiary.

In 1899, a long time after her father's death in 1883, Eleanor Marx edited and brought out as a book the pieces that Collet had published; but the book's tracing

of Britain's secret and corrupt relations with Russia as continuous for 150 years has usually been dropped from Marx's collected works in print, not least, as Francis Wheen has pointed out, for its necessary bypassing of the Crimean War. Clearly Marx regarded Urquhart as unreliable for the most part, but he also leapt at this chance to write about his hatred of Tsarist Russia and his suspicion of Palmerston. And despite some political differences, Marx and his family became close friends with the Collets.

Almost all the letters Marx wrote to Collet from the mid-1850s to the year before his death in 1883 were packed with detailed evidence of the sinister relations he believed existed between the British government and the Tsarist regime. They have more to do with the manipulations of the stock market − Barings, for instance, are distrusted as 'contractors' for the Russian government loan − and the iniquities of the press than with the diplomatic machinations which exercised Urquhart. Marx's handwriting grows smaller and more exquisite over the years, though it is never illegible; and he writes responsively and with much underlining and numbering of points, as if to someone picking his brains for information. There is a carefully laid out letter about the German electoral system, and there are others minutely summarising articles he had read about the stock market in either *Money Market Review* or *The Economist*. Marx was working on the first part of *Das Kapital* in the early 1860s − he later sent Collet a copy of the English and French editions − and the letters he wrote while he was working on the first volume enter dramatically and graphically into the spirit of the conspiracies he describes, delighting in the real-life detail of what he is discovering:

The difficulty, in such a case, for the B.o.E. [Bank of England] to come to a timely understanding with the government, and obtain at a moment's notice its relieving letter, may be judged from the avowal of the Governor of the B.o.E. that they had to act at an hour when the Chancellor of the Exchequer was probably still in the arms of Morpheus.

The Marxes became friends of the whole family, and Jane Collet and Jenny Marx organised those Shakespeare play-readings for their children, which were so enthusiastically recalled by Clara, and by Eleanor Marx in the letters she wrote to Collet about collecting copies of her father's articles in 1896. Clara remembered Marx as 'a kindly old man' and a 'good listener to us when Eleanor and Mrs Marx and I were chattering about the week's events at school or at the theatre'. Clara also recalled that 'my mother and elder sister never forgot an evening at the Marxes where one Frenchman proudly told my mother that everyone in the room was under sentence of death'. She had a memory of her own of one visit to the Marx household:

> All that remains to me is the memory of the little room full of people all talking French at the top of their voices. At that time and for thirty years or so I had the mistaken idea that when French people were talking like that they were quarrelling.

Another memory is of Marx helping her with her German homework, taking immense trouble with both the information she needed and the German in which she wrote it up. On another occasion, she tried out on him the points she was preparing to make against Brutus (versus Cassius) for a school debate about *Julius Caesar*:

> Every now and then K.M. nodded his head at quotations in support of my side. One remark of his, however, rather disconcerted me. I had accepted entirely the view that Brutus was disinterested and noble in character – but his leadership was none the better for that. K.M. remarked that in historical fact Brutus himself was accused of 'having an itching palm'.

'To Karl Marx,' she adds, 'Shakespeare's entirely English attitude to revolution by assassination given in *Julius Caesar* must have been of absorbing interest.'

Jane, meanwhile, was busy with the children and the laundry, and having difficulty with her ironers and their stubborn resistance to newfangled ideas. Her initially gleeful participation in her husband's political concerns suffered a setback, however – perhaps from experiencing them at close quarters, and particularly during the years when he was supporting the Urquhart cause. The draft of a letter addressed to an unidentified 'Dear Sir', which she probably never sent, expresses her exasperation with Collet's politics and his enthusiasms: 'The unaccountable infatuation with which he upholds Mr Urquhart's insane notions is a source of great uneasiness to all his nearest and dearest friends.'

One of his oldest friends was the slightly younger George Jacob Holyoake, famous for inventing the word 'secularism' and for spending six months in prison in 1842 for blasphemy. At the very end of his life he published a book with the endearing title *Bygones Worth*

Remembering. It was Holyoake who saw to it that the book Collet just managed to complete before his death, which happened a few days before his eighty-fifth birthday, would be published posthumously, with his encomium of its author as its Introduction. He also included as a frontispiece a photograph of Collet, inscrutably waiting for Dickens to memorialise him as an Aged P in his bow tie, stiff shirtfront and wavy layered lapels, his vast forehead and drooping eyelids framed by what look like tight curls. Holyoake writes of Collet's 'absolute disinterestedness' and 'scrupulous fairness to every Government with which we came in contact, and to heads of departments with whom unceasing war was waged'. It does seem that Collet was endowed with a remarkably sweet disposition for someone so given to political contention. He was certainly remembered as a charming father, 'Da' to them all, and the parent they wrote to when they were away from home. Away from home himself on her sixth birthday, Collet wrote to Carrie to tell her he had 'ordered your wheelbarrow and I hope you will find it in the bedroom on the morning of your birthday – He [the carpenter] promised to make it strong and I hope you will find great use and pleasure in it.' He went on to congratulate her for showing patience and forebearance with her three younger siblings and to warn her that she would need to cultivate those virtues even more assiduously in future years.

Collet believed firmly that his outsider and amateur status was fundamental to achieving his goals, and when Holyoake (perhaps surprisingly) asked him to write a character reference for his son Matthew, who was taking the Civil Service examination, Collet consented, of course, but also drafted on the back of Holyoake's letter his intended or perhaps only half-intended reply, which ran as follows:

> I cannot refuse to tell anybody who may ask me that Matthew's character is, to the best of my knowledge and belief, unexceptionable. I cannot, however, refrain from expressing to you my regret that the son of one who has earned an honourable name by resisting oppression, should have no nobler ambition than to live a life of inglorious ease as one of its tools. Of all the schemes that have been devised for ruining the nation the most mischievous is that for enticing the élite of its youth into the employment of the Government, so as to deprive the people of their natural leaders, and to uproot every barrier to the progress of corruption.

This was in 1865, before his own five children were anywhere near ready to consider careers for themselves. It seems likely, though, that he did feel some disappointment when two of his own children became civil servants. Times had changed by then, and their professional status came to mean as much to both Wilfred and Clara as Collet's amateur status had to him.

Collet's sister, Sophy, was nine years younger than he was. She was remembered as a precociously early talker and walker despite suffering from curvature of the spine, which crippled her and triggered a lifetime of illnesses, though she lived to be seventy-two and was remarkably active all her life. She was taught by her aunt Mary – partly at Miss Devall's school in Chelsea, where Mary taught and where Sophy's mother, Eliza, had taught too before her marriage

– but mostly on her own, at home. Aunt and niece kept up an almost daily correspondence all their lives, about books and music and God and the iniquities of slavery and racism in America and of capital punishment everywhere. Sophy was religious, differently so from all her relations, even from Aunt Mary, who took faith and Unitarianism for granted, admiring theologians and clerics who managed to be 'cheerful', 'amiable' and 'liberal' all at the same time; whereas religion had such importance for Sophy that for a time she even deserted Unitarianism, cast down by the absence of a human face from its deity. Could God rustle up enough sympathy and understanding for the human condition on his own, she wondered, without human guidance? In her youth, however, Unitarianism was a vital part of her life. She knew many of the leading figures in the Unitarian world of the South Place Chapel in Finsbury, where William Johnson Fox presided. Some of the transcriptions she made of his sermons were published, and she became friendly through him with the Flower sisters: Eliza, a musician and composer (who became Fox's second wife), and Sarah. She corresponded with James Martineau, Harriet's sometimes envied younger brother and a Unitarian divine, and when Richard Hutton, the once radical theologian, defected from Unitarianism to Anglicanism she took it personally.

Both Sophy and Mary read a great deal. Mary was nearly ninety when she wrote to her great-nephew Wilfred:

> I have just been reading the translation of a Latin work by Dante 'On Monarchy' – which I had never heard of till now – it is curious as coming from him, being an elaborate argument against the temporal authority of the Pope & and is placed at the end of a lecture or rather a studied Eulogium of Dante by Dr Church – a dry book but it contains some beautiful quotations.

Both Mary and Sophy composed music, mostly songs. Mary, for instance, wrote a song 'For Immigrants'. Sophy's songs were more likely to be hymns. Some of their work was published by Novello, and some of it performed locally at the South Place Chapel and other such venues. Both wrote for the *Spectator*, and Sophy wrote a column as 'Panthea' for Holyoake's the *Reasoner*, believing it her duty to argue against atheism from within the citadel, as it were; and she wrote some pieces for Emerson, whom she got to know during his visits to England. Mary couldn't get on with Emerson's writing, though, 'he gives me too much trouble'.

Mary was a beauty, and G. F. Watts drew her portrait

in elegant late middle age, while Sophy became progressively more crippled, a small hunched figure, though
not until she was actually dying did she make much of
her physical troubles in letters to anyone. Mary, born at
the end of the eighteenth century, knew Maria Edgeworth in her youth and encouraged a correspondence
between the young Sophy and her old friend. She taught
in her Chelsea school for many years and seems to have
formed romantic attachments to one or two of the young
women teachers there. Sophy taught the Holyoake children for a time, but she always hoped to make a living
from her writing. Both women must have survived on
very little money and both lived alone for much of their
lives; though when Mary retired from teaching she lived
in Bath with a Mrs Dawson, of whom she was clearly
very fond, while Sophy lived uneasily at times with her
mother, but more often on her own.

A Rowland Hill, presumably the son of Collet's old
headmaster, wrote to Sophy's niece Edith when Sophy

died in 1894: 'She had a masculine intellect and a great comprehensive heart and was the best friend India ever had in England.' I can't help hoping that Sophy would have found Hill's faith in the superiority of the masculine intellect surprising in relation to herself. She was certainly capable of giving some masculine intellects quite a pasting. Carlyle was capable at times of writing 'insane folly', and here she is on Thoreau's *Walden, or Life in the Woods*:

> A most disappointing medley of the saintly and the silly, not wholly without a strong spice of the selfish. Mr Thoreau is a sort of Emerson-gone-mad, a transcendentalist who is wholly centrifugal, and who has thrown off all thought of boundaries or measure. He describes no elliptical orbit, but runs off into an eternal hyperbola. In plainer terms, he does not believe in society, he sees only <u>individual</u> life, and holds every relationship, whether to family or mankind, as next to worthless. Such a folly is to be regretted much, for its <u>apparent</u> agreement with high and heroic instincts gives it a charm for those men whose force of character would make them valuable leaders in elevating the tone of social life. Yet I think the unparalleled absurdities in this book will prevent it from doing any great mischief.

Nor was she much kinder, it has to be admitted, to certain women novelists, including Charlotte Brontë:

> How writers of any ambition can stoop to waste themselves on that sort of light stuff, unless it be

for bread, I can't think. It whiles away a headache or amuses an hour or so very well, but it's like eating puff-pastry – a few agreeable sensations, and there's an end. There is a terrible absence of <u>purpose</u> in the literary world. Then again, those graceful woman-novels, Florence Templar, 'Thorney Hall', etc, they are merely autobiographies of the affections <u>purs et simples</u>. The heroines love, and would prefer being beloved in turn, if it be possible – if not, they make the best of it, but in either case, they have no life of their own, no purpose beyond the affections, no aspirations except a vague desire to be good. How <u>can</u> women be so easily contented, so torpid? Oh! for strength to live out something fuller and nobler without forgetting the restraining grace of true womanhood.

'How different from that lovely Mrs Gaskell, no less strong [than Charlotte Brontë, that is] but so much more womanly,' she went on to say. I can't help wishing that she had not felt it necessary to end her fulminations on quite that note, or wondering what intelligent women like these really wanted and hoped for for women. Did they console themselves with thoughts of 'the restraining grace of true womanhood'? And did they feel themselves to be possessed of it? Sophy corresponded for years with the well-known feminist writer Frances Power Cobbe, and when they disagreed, as they did quite vehemently at times, it was about religion (Cobbe had no time for it) rather than women's prospects. There is no doubt of Sophy's as well as Mary's commitment to educating girls; and Sophy's earliest interest in India took the form of support for the setting-up of schools for

Indian girls in Calcutta. But as an article of political faith, the issue of women's rights was more openly espoused by the men they knew. For Collet, it was always part of any programme he argued for, though given less than top priority; and for Francis Newman, younger brother of the cardinal, and for many years in regular correspondence with Sophy, 'the uprising of woman-hood is the grandest event of this century, and I shall die thanking God for it'.

Newman was an important figure in Sophy's life. Handsome and emotional and interested in many of the same things as she was, he also slipped £5 notes for her into some of his letters. He had moved in the opposite direction from his older brother in terms of both religion and politics, becoming a teacher of Latin at University College London and, ultimately, a Unitarian. Newman approached Sophy warily at first as the reviewer of a book of his in the atheist *Reasoner*. Later, he appears to have sent her books to review for the *Spectator*. Their letters eventually covered a lot of ground: the American Civil War and efforts to abolish slavery, his brother's move towards Rome and what Francis believed to be the cardinal's hatred of Protestantism. There was Francis's own writing about 'Theism', Frances Cobbe's 'theories' of Unitarianism, which both Newman and Sophy disputed, and, finally, India. Both were concerned about the high-handedness of the British presence in India and Britain's insensitivity to India's cultural and religious traditions. Newman put it, a little cryptically, like this in an 1874 letter to Sophy:

> I sometimes think that nothing but an upsetting of aristocratic rule in England will suffice to reconcile either Ireland or India to us. On the other hand, any critical struggle in England is likely to precipitate revolutionary effort in both Ireland & India.

Sophy was to go further in engaging with India and Indians. She first saw Rammohun Roy, the famous Bengali reformer, at South Place Chapel when she was ten. Whether from that moment or later, she developed an astonishing knowledge of Indian religion and culture, was extremely well informed about the British presence there and came to know well a number of Indians, who visited her in London. The book she eventually wrote, *The Life and Letters of Raja Rammohun Roy*, is a strange and illuminating document, made odder by a final chapter written by 'a friend', Herbert Stead, after her death, which appears to contradict some of her own arguments in earlier chapters. She claims at the beginning of the book that it was Roy's 'religious personality' that mattered most to her, more even than the doctrinal and political struggles she goes on to unravel. The study she made of Roy, and of the movement within Hinduism, the Brahmo Somaj, that he brought about, occupied the last twenty years of her life. She taught herself Bengali in order to read into contemporary debates within Hinduism and in order to read Roy's translations into Bengali of the old Vedanta scriptures in Sanskrit. She must always have known that she would never have the strength to go to India herself, and her extraordinary achievement was to have written about this man and this movement, in the context of Bengali life in the early nineteenth century, from the seclusion of a series of rented rooms in North London, and to have been considered, by several Indian experts in the field, 'the greatest authority on the contemporary history of this movement'.

Rammohun Roy, a Brahmin from a rich, educated family, was born in a village in Bengal in 1772 and died and was buried in Bristol in 1833. Though Sophy occasionally alludes to Roy's arrogance and even vanity, she clearly found 'the great Hindu', as she sometimes called him in her book, a figure of romance as well as gravitas, whose early 'heresies', particularly those which opposed 'suttee' (the burning of widows) and child marriages, won her utmost respect. He began to question central aspects of Hinduism when he was still young and was inspired to do so as much by his growing interest in Christianity, and especially in a more or less Unitarian form of Christianity, as by his horror of all manifestations of 'idolatry', as Sophy expresses it. Her book may be read as a repository of genuine efforts made on both sides to reconcile Indian and Western philosophical ideas,

but it also bears the traces of British society's endemic racism in Sophy's day and of the kinds of challenge such racism provoked. So that in her admiration for Roy and her passionate desire to demonise all opposition to him, she allowed herself to forget the traditions of intellectual debate and tolerance that had characterised aspects of Bengali life for generations and which had also in some sense produced Roy himself. She could write a passage like this:

> Thick clouds of ignorance and superstitition hung over all the land; the native Bengali public had few books, and no newspapers. Idolatry was universal, and was often of a most revolting character; poly-

gamy and infanticide were prevalent, and the lot of Bengali women was too often a tissue of ceaseless oppressions and miseries, while as the crowning horror, the flames of the suttee were lighted with almost incredible frequency even in the immediate vicinity of Calcutta.

But she could also point out that Roy chose a Unitarian place of worship because he could be sure that there at least 'he heard nothing of Incarnation, Union of Two Natures, or Trinity, – doctrines which he regarded as only a variant of the anthropomorphic and polytheistic mythology of popular Hinduism'. Few religions, Sophy believed, and so, it seems, did Roy, could escape charges of 'idolatry'.

Her achievement was to perceive Roy's dilemma as a tension between the attractions for him of Christianity and Western culture, on the one hand, and on the other the pressures there were to deliver a revitalised Hinduism, a mystical, modern, even monotheistic version of Hinduism, based on his own translations of the Sanskrit Vedanta into Bengali and offered as a return to the true, the original Hinduism. Sophy appears to have understood the kinds of resistance he must have met with in Bengal to any criticism of Hindu practices which appeared to invoke Christianity or British mores or the various missionary operations in Bengal at the time. The interest of her book lies in her ability to record and understand the reasons for the failure to establish Unitarianism in Calcutta, a failure which explained and was responsible for the establishment and growth of the Brahmo Somaj in Bengal.

★   ★   ★

By the time Sophy died in 1894, her nephew Wilfred
had spent several years in Fiji in the Colonial Service,
and was married with one son. Another son would be
born in the following year, but his third, my father, would
not be born for another eleven years. Clara had already
been at the Board of Trade for two years as 'Labour
Correspondent', with special responsibility for women's
industrial conditions. They were a new generation,
looking towards a new century and the end of the
Victorian era. Wilfred wrote to his father from Fiji,
sending news of naval balls and bands and dysentery, but

also pointing out the need to 'put down' intertribal warfare and the arms and liquor and labour (he sometimes calls it the 'slave') trades. His letter reminds one of the scale and effort of maintaining the Empire and the boredom and hardship suffered by the colonisers as well as the colonised. Those tiny islands, almost invisible on any map of the Pacific Ocean, barely had harbours then, and where they had they were breeding grounds for malaria. Yet Wilfred manages to sound as if he's in the thick of it, and perhaps that was what you needed to think as you trained the brass band and kept an eye on 'the natives' at the other end of the earth. He rebukes his father for suggesting that it might be worth giving up the Falkland Islands in exchange for the New Hebrides. It would be 'like giving a whale for a herring'. His father is also put right about the amateurish Robert Louis Stevenson, 'a meddling, conceited fool, who thinks as a successful novelist he should be allowed to try to rule Samoa'.

Clara experienced her own version of being simultaneously in the thick of it and on the edges. Sometimes the only woman on a committee at the heart of government, she was also battling to employ one married woman graduate and to be heard on the subject of a minimum wage for home workers. Her family, consistently irritating but endlessly interesting too, turned her into an archivist, and for years she played with the letters and papers she had inherited. She transcribed great swathes of them, a correspondence between two women cousins in the eighteenth century, for instance; and letters from her ancestor Samuel Collet in the 1720s, prefiguring his own and his family's moves towards what would come to be thought of as Unitarian beliefs. She published some of these letters as pamphlets, with not much comment, as if she could not quite get a purchase on their significance, whether for herself or for some kind of history she might have imagined writing about the Dissenting middle classes. However, she clearly enjoyed her ancestor's outpourings of advice, about the kinds of women his sons should marry:

> One further hint I would give you in the choice of a Wife; avoid the two Extreams, a Melancholy, & a Witty Woman; the first will be no Wife at all, the last a Wife for all the World, which I think is the worst character in Life, & I am sure must make a good man Miserable.

And later, when one of his sons had in fact just become married for the third time, about how to keep the marriage alive:

> As you are blessed with a truly pious wife I recommend to you & her reading together a dream on the advantages of the married state sold by Keith in Gracechurch Street price twopence.

He interspersed such advice with suggestions about investments and warnings about the need to avoid the least taint of the 'trinitarian'. Clara may also have enjoyed this patriarch's brand of proto-Zionism or millenarianism. In 1747, he published *A Treatise of the Future Restoration of the Jews and Israelites to their own Land*. There had been and continued to be a tradition in this English family of somewhat offhand sympathy for Jews and objections to at least the grosser manifestations of anti-semitism.

Towards the end of her life, Clara pruned and privately published the letters her grandfather John Dobson had written to his cousin Eliza Barker (they were to become Collet and Sophy's parents) during the four years before their marriage in 1810. She called the volume, with characteristic edge, *The Letters of John to Eliza. A Four Years' Correspondence Course in the Education of Women. 1806–1810.* John's letters survived, presumably because Eliza kept them. Hers to him did not. Her later letters to her children and to her sister, however, of which a great many survive, are affectionately humdrum. Sometimes, John's letters read like love letters to the eighteen-year-old cousin he is preparing for marriage to him, though they are rather uneasy love letters, for he clearly wondered at times whether his future bride was really good enough for him. He writes as a hopeful young businessman of twenty-seven, beginning to establish himself in shipping and overseas trade, and his serial sermons to this young woman are a good deal more practical and down-to-earth than James Fordyce's *Sermons to Young Women*, where his readers are told to remember that their 'business chiefly is to read Men'. As John writes to Eliza, with his own brand of egotistical logic, 'It is only in the event that you can avail yourself of opportunities to cultivate your mind, that I can rationally hope to make you permanently happy.'

John is writing to a young teacher. Eliza and her sister Mary, four years younger than she is, were assistant teachers at Miss Devall's school in Cadogan Place, Chelsea. This does not encourage him to regard Eliza as in any way his equal, and he is not reticent in offering his advice on virtually every aspect of her life: on shoes and hats and dresses; on health and the benefits to it of walks and dancing; on grammar and usage and style and what she ought to read to keep them in good repair; on travel and the miracles of inoculation and on how to negotiate a pay rise without seeming greedy. He assumes that she will have a globe or atlas as well as a dictionary by her side at all times, and particularly while she is reading his letters. It is her duty to teach the children in her school and his, as he sees it, to teach her. His letters may be read, as his granddaughter Clara suggests, as a textbook, and Eliza seems sometimes to have found them wearisome. They come accompanied by books and papers and magazines – the *Edinburgh Review* and the *Weekly Messenger*, for instance – and always there are detailed instructions about how to read and about the good that will come from doing so. He sends her two volumes of Maria Edgeworth's stories.

> Keep them by you dear Girl, and now and then *when your heart* is so disposed read *one* of them. I send the Popular Tales with them which are also as excellent as the others. I have added two small volumes of poetry by Bowles which you have already seen but which I wish you at your leisure to *enjoy* – do not however in attending to the agreeable, forget the useful – study the Scientific Dialogues with steady and unwearied attention untill you find yourself completely mistress of them. Never take them up when you are not perfectly disposed for them – and never suffer anything to pass until you understand it – *it does not signify how little you acquire at a time provided that be accurately*

acquired – do not disturb yourself if you should find you have forgotten what you had once acquired – *it is for a time the case with everybody* – begin again – if you meet with anything you cannot clearly comprehend give me the page and subject and I will try to render it more clear to you.

The pedagogic tone is unrelenting and unacknowledged. John is pleased to think of Eliza as a teacher and admits that he would never have the patience to work with children himself, whereas 'it is extremely pleasant to me to think of you as interested about children'. He wants her to dress fashionably and take an interest in her clothes, but he is also certain that 'there is much more Economy in your qualifying yourself to direct the Education of your children should you be blessed with any than there would be in saving the expense of making your new stock of Cloathes'. In fact, they were to have seven children, though John did not live to see any of them grown up. Here, he links Eliza's current work as a teacher with her future responsibilities as a mother, picturing her surrounded by the children she teaches, and imagining her passing on and reading aloud to them information from the books and newspapers he supplies her with:

Indeed I do conceive that you might very much increase your powers of usefulness & the interest you would take in many of the articles . . . were you to read them to the children you are fond of. Surely the little Girl who took so much delight in hearing Miss B . . . talk about Astronomy would love to listen to her – and would you not delight to fill their little minds with truths and drive away those prejudices which you say sometimes disturb you.

Provoked at times by her apparent complacency and by her unwillingness to tell him her innermost thoughts, he sometimes criticises her, for 'ludicrous blunders' in her letters, for using 'get' rather than 'become' and 'that' as an expletive. Quite early in their correspondence he writes frankly of his misgivings:

> I will confess to you that I am sensible you are deficient in many of those accomplishments which are universally considered of some importance to a female. You do not sing, or play, or paint, or speak Italian, or write French with fluency – you possess no extraordinary taste in dress – converse very little – are neglectful of the trifling forms & ceremonies which are thought essential in society – and would not shine particularly in cutting up a goose for a large party at the head of your own *table*, nor in doing the general business of it. I am further sensible that although you have read much, it has been in a desultory manner (without any plan) . . . I am aware that you are not a perfect beauty – that there are figures much more graceful than yours is. I know that your constitution is indifferent – that it is such as to incline you naturally to be indolent and that I must expect you to be frequently unwell . . . I think I hear you almost breathless cry out Stop – and ask me how I ever could have told you 'you were exquisitely dear to me – that I was satisfied with you and that you had more than answered

all my expectations?' – I said so, my dear Friend, because I felt it was the truth – and I believe it still.

She seems to have taken the huff, and his concluding sentiment did not let him off. Nor was this the last time he offended her. Eventually, he bought a grand piano for her future use, after four years of nagging her to practise, and to practise playing 'good' music rather than bad, indeed 'scientific' music rather than the simple tunes she was used to, by which he seems to have meant the more complex counterpoint of Handel and Haydn. There are harangues on poetry, on taste, on science and mathematics and on being au fait with foreign affairs. These were the years of Napoleon's dominion over most of Europe, and John's business took him abroad, most often to Malta. Perhaps he had come across Coleridge there in 1804, trying to come off opium. Years later, John's granddaughter Clara's sparingly used editorial pencil is wielded only to amputate some longish tirades on electricity, magnetism and other modern marvels.

I imagine Clara publishing these letters out of a double sense of their interest. Partly, she wanted to illustrate the historical fact that the education of women had been taken seriously in Unitarian families and that it was an education for real life, by and large, rather than for social accomplishments or even intellectual benefit; but she also used them to emphasise the contradictions, as she perceived them, in educating women beyond a certain point if they were to marry and have children. She once made it clear to her nephew, my father, that she much preferred her great-aunt Mary to her grandmother, Eliza, who successfully resisted most of her future husband's

efforts to educate her. Mary, who did not marry and lived to the age of ninety-four, was a woman after Clara's own heart, a woman of intellect, sense and spirit. John is gently mocked for his consistently pedagogic tone. Eliza, however, is despaired of for having no intellectual interests of her own.

Samuel Richardson's *Pamela* is not one of the novels John recommends to Eliza, though it is hard to believe she did not read it anyway. The peculiar wooing Eliza received might well have provided her with interpretative tactics for reading Richardson's novel. For in contrast to John's unflagging transmission of his own views on matrimony and the role and duties of women, Richardson imagined the woman herself and literally gave voice to her struggle to become the mother and teacher who would be seen to vindicate, through her enchanting and enchanted submission, the limitations set on her own education and the efficacy of a regime organised to produce men and to control the influence women might have on them.

That tradition of men advising women on the principles of modern childcare and education goes back even further in Clara's family. More than fifty years before John started writing to Eliza, in 1752 (twelve years after *Pamela* was published and ten years before Rousseau's *Emile* burst upon the world), a great-uncle shared by John and Eliza, called Joseph Collet, wrote three long letters to his future sister-in-law, Sarah Lasswell (John and Eliza's shared grandmother), apparently in response to her request for his 'Opinion on that most Difficult Subject the Education of Children'. Clara had these typed and must have wanted to do something with them. Neither Joseph nor Sarah had children of their own when the letters were written (Joseph – son of old Samuel and recipient of those torrents of advice from him on the subject of marriage – was the son who married three times), so one may presume that experience was not an essential qualification for offering or receiving advice of this kind. It seems likely that Joseph (like Richardson's Pamela) would have read John Locke's *Some Thoughts Concerning Education*, and that he was influenced by a need to adumbrate a different educational regime, not intended for Locke's 'young Gentleman', but for the sons of Dissenting middle-class families. The letters suggest that rationality, moderation and good sense are the essential qualities for child-rearing, that education is principally a family responsibility, and that the chief hazards faced by young children are likely to be at the hands of nurses and servants and mothers. Childhood had not yet been marked out as a separate terrain, requiring a specially trained workforce, and whereas Locke focuses on the figure of the tutor, Joseph Collet regards the family, and especially the father, as primarily responsible for a boy's education.

The letters move through the years of the child's growing up (predictably, the child is a boy), so that the first letter takes him to five or six and the establishment of good habits, through kindly persuasion and truthfulness. There will be early formal teaching of the alphabet, numbers, world geography, the reading of moral stories and fables and a concentration on children's developing habits of care, accuracy and attention. Punishment is to be avoided. It is clear in a number of ways that this is an upbringing designed for children growing up in the Dissenting middle class of the mid-eighteenth century: it is anti-aristocratic, anti-classical, liberal in some respects, in favour of French and Dutch (the mercantile languages of the period, though an earlier generation of the family put Portuguese before French) rather than Latin and Greek. These, Joseph insists, are fine for children 'if you design them for Law, Physick or Divinity', but certainly not otherwise:

> I could wish our School learning for young Gentlemen from 10 or 12 years of age to their prenticeships was Carry'd on in a Different manner than it is at present. Of what use can be their reading Ovid and many other Heathen authors but to Learn their Superstitions, and what Service can all their Nonsense of their Gods and Godesses amours, dissensions, Battles &c. be of but only to fill Children's Tender minds with foolish Ideas, Ridiculous fancys, Idle Superstitions and above all (as they are growing

to an age so susceptible of and Inclinable to Amorous desires) Their Lewd and Wanton Storys must Infallibly tend to the blowing up the Sparks of Lust and Impurity which it is one great design of Education to damp and extinguish; How much better would it be if some books of Christian morality were read in the place of those heathen authors.

In Joseph Collet's universe, children will be encouraged to show kindness and generosity to the poor, though they must also learn early to distinguish the industrious poor from beggars, to whom they should not give money (a principle adhered to with disconcerting enthusiasm by Clara 140 years later in her support for the Charity Organisation Society). The concentration here is on the education of boys, for it is through boys and then through men as fathers that family order and happiness are to be achieved.

How Happy is the Father of an Orderly and Well Govern'd Family. He acts as a King in his own house and sees his Laws Chearfully and punctually obey'd, as they are not the effects of meer Arbitrary will and absolute Power but wise, usefull and necessary to the Hapiness of every one of his Children.

By the age of ten or eleven – as the third letter asserts – the purpose of education is preparation for a future when the young 'must soon quit their fathers House and go into the wide World, the young men to their prenticeship and the young ladys to be mistresses of familys Themselves'. And these families are the model of order and sense, with the father presiding as inspiration for and regulator of a regime of relative permissiveness. The historian Rosalind Mitchison has reminded us of just how relative an emphasis on individualism and permissiveness was likely to be in the middle of the eighteenth century:

> Individualism may mean permissiveness. In the reaction to both formalism and puritanism it often did. But it could also mean the expression of the personality of the father at the expense of everyone else . . . The private person with whom Locke's political thought was concerned was an adult male landowner. No one else counted as an individual, certainly not a servant, an employee, a woman.

Joseph Collet was not a landowner, but he was a man of his time. He did not altogether ignore the education of girls. A final image from his letters may be thought to anticipate Clara's contrasting memories of her own childhood in North London, reading Shakespeare with her brothers and sisters and the younger daughters of Karl Marx:

> Where there are several young Ladies in a family it is a very Good Method to let the Eldest read for an Hour whilst the rest work and then the Second take it for another hour and the eldest sit down to work, and so on till each has read Her hour. Thus they'll Improve in reading and working at once, and have food for the mind as well as Employment for the hands, and when your son is at home and can be spared from other Studys or bussiness, Let

him read to them (as of an Evening) whilst all the Ladies work. The books to be Chosen are such as will both divert and Instruct as Telemachus and the Travels of Cyrus, Love makes a Man, the provoked Husband, and Cato are the best Romances and plays I know of, but I should be very Carefull of these sort of books. Good History, as Prideauxs Connection of ye old and New Testamts, Echards Eclesiastical History, Rollins Roman and Antient History, Rapins History of England &c. are what I should prefer, as giving us a real account of things and not filling the mind with foolish Romantick Ideas, without any foundation in truth, but of all books for young Ladies I prefer the Spectators Tatlers and Guardians, as soon as ever they are capable of understanding them.

Carefully marked out here are the purposes and limitations of a woman's education, the uses to which it might be put, its domestication within the family, with reading as an accompaniment to useful and profitable activity rather than as an end in itself. There is the separation of the male and female economies of space and time: the time spent (or all too easily wasted) by women is compared with the time used gainfully by men. Even the care of young children, if it is taken seriously and done with a clear sense of outcome, is better performed by men. It is possible to trace much of Clara's belief in the need for a practical and moral education for working-class girls back to this well-developed tradition of educational thinking in the middle of the eighteenth century.

There may well be less of Matthew Arnold's 'sweetness and light' in Clara's inheritance than the 'energy, self-reliance, and capital' Arnold warned against, though I have difficulties, I have to admit, with such a distinction. Clara grew up in a family and within a tradition where women took advantage of every opportunity to develop their talents and to make an impact on a world they understood to be full of poverty and injustice, and especially so for many women. Almost exactly 150 years after Joseph Collet wrote his letters to Sarah Lasswell, Clara registered her own sense of history and change:

> Our pioneers were full of enthusiasm in their journey to the promised land where sex barriers should be removed and sex prejudices die away. Those of us who passed through the gates which they opened for us were (I am afraid it must be admitted) often unpopular among those we left behind and were delighted with the novelty of the country before us. The next generation are coming into the field under new conditions. To begin with, it is realised that work is work; next, that economic liberty is only obtained by the sacrifice of personal freedom; that there is nothing very glorious in doing work that any average man can do as well, now that we are no longer told we cannot do it. The glamour of economic independence has faded, although the necessity for it is greater than ever.

I have found myself looking to women of Clara's generation for solidarity, a sense of historical continuity, even some recognition of what life might be like fifty or more years after her death. One of her short stories, written in her thirties and dealing with 'the woman question', ends with the words, 'The nineteenth century has propounded the problem, perhaps the twentieth century may solve it.' There is certainly no triumphalism in anything she wrote and she was never given to Utopian visions. There is, though, concentrated reflection on just how far things had changed and just how much there was still to do.

Outside and In

I began this book during the last year of my mother's life. It was a way of registering that bit of both our lives as tethered to the rest. Obituaries and letters of condolence tactfully avoid mentioning failure, disappointment, loss of power. Yet most deaths, especially those of the very old, are accompanied by thoughts of futility and waste, even if those thoughts may go unmentioned as the dying do their dying and the living reflect on the curious business of staying alive, surviving, having more life to live. Scalded at times by the heat of tensions among my living relations, it was an unexpected pleasure to re-enter the world of my dead ones through the memories of my dying mother and to begin to wonder what my relations with these families had really been. Was this where I belonged? I have never felt explained by them. Nor have I always felt able to explain them. I learn something when I examine the past and imagine the youth of those I remember in their old age; for the old feel closer to their own youth than the young can ever believe.

In one of the books she wrote in the late 1970s about her own and her family's experience of emigration and division, Maxine Hong Kingston let out a cry of bewilderment:

Chinese-Americans, when you try to understand what things in you are Chinese, how do you separate what is peculiar to childhood, to poverty, insanities, one family, your mother who marked your growing with stories, from what is Chinese? What is Chinese tradition and what is the movies?

How *do* children sort that out? How do adults? Do questions like these persist and remain unanswered for ever as we bed down more or less uncomfortably within the descriptions our families provide for themselves and for us? And is it inevitable that we should experience the two families we most immediately spring from as separate, in conflict? Without division and uncertainty of that sort, undeniably there from the beginning and essential to who we might be or become, we might be lost, surely, crazily believing in – even expecting to find – the existence somewhere of unity, purity, perfection, and quite unable to tolerate opposites, alternatives, dissension.

I have known very young children use the words 'normal' and 'normally' well before getting their farmyard animals straight. 'Is my family normal?' is the natural precursor to 'Am I normal?' and is closely followed, one may hope, by 'What is normal, and would I want to be it if I knew what it was?' Perhaps our particular experiences of class and race and religious difference stay with us as benchmarks for all the questions we inevitably go on asking about normality and its opposites and about all those things we simultaneously take for granted and remain astonished by.

Both sides of my family differed from many others in keeping records, family trees, letters, documents, photographs. Some have been confidently offered for storage in university libraries. More have been stuffed into used brown envelopes or tied in bundles with string or pink ribbon and left to the mice and the damp in a series of lofts and attics. You would have to say that any family that keeps its written debris quite so assiduously and for so many years must have been urged on by some kind of self-importance, and possibly as well by an unusually long-term experience and expectation of physical security and stability. Maxine Hong Kingston's family lost everything on their translation from China to California, and her books set out to remake a past from the traces she picked up from stories and her own memories.

I, on the contrary, have had letters and books and short stories and wills and diaries to go on, and a great-aunt who transcribed and even published whole chunks of the archive she put together and passed on, though she never explained why she was doing it. Perhaps she was as puzzled by the idea of families as I have sometimes been. She filled dozens of notebooks with her discoveries of adventurers, students, miscreants, provincial worthies, bluestockings, who happened to share her name (and mine), and she even claimed Dean Colet of St Paul's as an ancestor – a celibate and childless one, I assume – who seems to have inherited a 'vast fortune' from his father. So where did that go? I notice that she didn't complain about *his* spelling. And I haven't read anything like all there is to read of Clara's uncoverings. Some of the letters she preserved are overwritten or cross-written to save paper, or are simply illegible, and I have had to pretend to myself that anything I couldn't read was probably not worth reading. What would a real historian do, I wonder? I confess that I have been swept by warm gusts of affection for those whose handwriting could be easily deciphered: Karl Marx especially, but also my father and mother.

Several things separated my two families: religion and money, most obviously. Yet for three centuries they have both been English families, firmly settled into opposite corners of the English middle class. The distance between my mother and father as individuals could be said to have exceeded by a good deal the distance between their families, at least so far as their children and grandchildren were concerned. Temperament, interests, looks, gender, their childhood landscapes and the contents of their minds and memories: these separated them for me more dramatically than class or culture or money did. And what probably kept them together was their shared view of art as a calling which sets you apart from class, family and so on.

But that was disingenuous of them, and perhaps I am being disingenuous too: for despite its capaciousness and elasticity, the English middle class has offered a nourishing site for flowerings of snobbery and fine class distinctions. The Collets and the Salamans were the beneficiaries of that ambivalence or indeterminacy about class on which the English have insisted, even seeming to find it good for the soul. And both families experienced themselves as outsiders. Clara – romantically, I think – described her family's class as

> Anglo-Norman sea traders or merchant adventurers
> accustomed to months of isolation on the high seas
> and to lonely years of mercantile business in remote
> seaports surrounded by populations to whom they
> were alien in race and religion.

She was thinking of old Joseph Collet of the East India Company, the rebuilder and Governor of Fort St George

in Madras. India provided his side of the family with considerable wealth (though he had gone there to escape and recover from bankruptcy), and when he came back to England in 1720, he did so under some sort of financial cloud, though he bought or rented Hertford Castle and lived there with his family until his death in 1725. His younger brother Samuel, on the other hand, from whom both Clara and I are descended, had stayed at home to become a fairly prosperous merchant (possibly a skinner, though I don't know what he skinned), prosperous enough to retire early and devote himself to writing extremely long poems of a Miltonic cast and engage in theological argument. His garden in Greenwich was full of grapes, 'three sorts of strawberries' and a riot of other fruit and vegetables, which he dispensed to his family along with his homilies. His largesse on all fronts alternated with expressions of weakness and vulnerability, until his oldest son, John the doctor, moved him to Newbury to be close to his own family and practice. Here Samuel waited noisily to die, exasperated by age and diminution and finding everything around him simultaneously dwindling and expensive: the harvest, especially, 'sadly laid and the sheaves light'.

I have the strong sense that Clara's father, Collet Dobson Collet, Samuel's great-great-grandson and my great-grandfather, would have laughed at anyone who worried so incessantly about God's plans for us all, let alone about whether he and his ancestors counted as gentlemen. He'd have been happy to concede, I think, that he and his family had come down in the world in some respects – no bad thing, he would have felt. He married a Scottish woman, however, who felt that she was marrying into a different class as well as a different culture and language, and perhaps she was. She was remembered not for her class but for her sense and practicality. Her laundry, and the houses she bought and rented out, must have paid the school bills and eventually subsidised her children's earnings, for they all earned their livings.

The Salamans were rentiers on an altogether grander scale, and once upon a time there was even something called the Salaman Estates. I knew this because for some years a goose arrived at Christmas in a sack with an emerald-green label telling us so. Mismanagement as well as Second World War bombing lost the family most of this prime London property (a lot of it in Notting Hill Gate), until an emerald-green label hanging from a hook on our kitchen dresser was all there was left to remind us of past glories. I grew up, nonetheless, thinking of the Salaman family as richer and therefore grander than the Collets. My grandfather and his brothers and sisters lived in big country houses. Jewishness added to their glamour and superiority, as far as I was concerned, though a consideration of how these families might have thought of themselves and each other in, say, 1870, reminds me of my innocence in these matters. It took me a long time to associate anti-semitism with anything my family might ever have experienced. Nor did I see any objection to the idea that you could be 100 per cent English and 100 per cent Jewish at the same time. This raised issues of quantity, but not of identity. Many English Jewish families just as well established in England as the Salamans were converted to Christianity during the eighteenth and nineteenth centuries or became gradually assimilated. Others, through old wealth and their unofficial position as lay leaders of the Jewish community, managed to live like English country gentlemen while maintaining fairly good relations with the growing Jewish population in London and other cities, most of whom came from Germany and Russia between the last decades of the nineteenth century and the beginning of the Second World War. Todd Endelman has written of my grandfather:

> It was not wealth alone, however, that sustained Salaman's connection to Anglo-Jewry and underwrote his willingness to participate in its governance. Just as decisive were the circumstances of his upbringing. Salaman came of age at a moment in Anglo-Jewish history in which ethnic and family

ties were more important than observance and belief in forging Jewish solidarity at the upper levels of the community. He never outgrew the impress of these circumstances. His 'Victorian' commitments – to civility, noblesse oblige, fraternity, charity – remained intact until his death at mid-century. But the world around him changed.

Perhaps there is some elaborate algebraic formula that would permit me to express intelligible equivalences and distinctions between these two families and their social position, while taking into account money, property, land, earning power, but also history, religion, education, even style. All I can say is that I never wanted to see my father's aunts confronting or confronted by my Jewish grandfather or his children. I had reason to fear a stand-off, some pretty expert upstaging on both sides, and I would have been mortified by that. These families shared more than they would have acknowledged. They were confident, educated, middle-class people, who experienced themselves – though differently – as outsiders and were mostly able to turn this to good account.

But then I have also been astonished to discover just how important religion was for each family's sense of itself and of its difference from other families. I am astonished because I have only the most negative feelings about religion. For one or two individuals in both my families, religion was something that infused and inspired their lives. My grandmother Nina was passionately and persuasively Jewish, for instance, and old Samuel Collet, 'the Patriarch', as he was known to later generations, was a veritable ancient mariner, a professional button-holer, who was even given a huge silver tankard in 1717 by Caroline, Princess of Wales, for giving 'The Best Oration on Good Will to Men'. He and his great-great-granddaughter (my great-great-aunt) Sophy were such profoundly 'religious personalities' that everything they wrote or thought about was somehow lit by this as by a nimbus. Religion was not only a matter of faith and spiritual need for all three, it was an intoxication, with theology, philosophy, argument and, for my Jewish grandmother and for old Samuel Collet, poetry as well. Sophy once wrote in her niece Clara's 'Confessions Album' that her favourite occupation was 'writing theology'. For almost all the other members of both families religion mattered because it defined who you were and who you weren't. It accounted for how you brought up and educated your children, for who you married and what work you did and the people you knew, and for how you were likely to think about public and political events of the day and about change and what needed to happen – and what you needed to do – to make the world a better place.

If religion has somehow defined both families' sense of themselves, education was what brought them together, though the Dissenting Collets had a traceable history of concern with education going back to the beginning of the eighteenth century and no doubt before that, whereas it seems likely that the Salamans reached the same point much later and by another route. My parents met through Bedales, which I have characterised before as the oldest and by now probably the least radical or experimental of the co-educational and so-called 'progressive' boarding schools in England. My Salaman grandfather sent all his children there, a reaction, perhaps, to his own unhappy time at St Paul's; while my father was taken away from another London boys' school when he was twelve or so, because he had been ill and perhaps because his father and his aunts felt he needed country air and company of his own age. About thirty members of both families have been to Bedales. Even now one or two second or third cousins are to be found there, I imagine on scholarships – it is one of the most expensive schools in the country – and wrestling, as I did, with their under-exercised consciences as they receive a schooling so benevolent and upbeat as to deprive them of what might be thought useful grit and difficulty, and certainly of any understanding of what schooling is like for most children. My father taught at Bedales for about eight years, though there was a longish gap in the middle, and my sisters and I were given free places as a result.

Both families have made use of another educational institution: University College London. Founded in 1826 by a committee consisting of Dissenters, Utilitarians, Whigs and, pivotally, the Jewish Isaac Goldsmid, and called by its many enemies at the time 'The Cockney College', University College made it possible for Catholics, Jews, Dissenters and eventually women to have a university education for the first time. My great-grandfather, Collet Dobson Collet, went there as a student in 1832. He was followed by his son Wilfred and his daughter Clara, who became the first woman fellow of the college, and eventually by my father. My Jewish great-grandfather, Myer, who left school at thirteen and made a fortune, went to evening classes there while he was learning to run the family business. My husband ran the English department at UCL for many years, and my brother-in-law trained as a doctor and taught there for a bit too, while several great-aunts and uncles and my mother and one of my sons were students at the Slade, the fine art department of the same college. University College was not only hospitable to those who were unwelcome in the older universities, it supported and developed versions of scholarship and teaching which have modernised the curriculum and challenged the privilege and domination of Oxford and Cambridge.

Nonetheless, once Jews were allowed at Cambridge, my grandfather went there, the first member of his family to go to university. He was followed by three of his children, eight or nine of his grandchildren and at least as many of his great-grandchildren, just as many of them girls as boys. Only my father went to Cambridge from his side of the family, though Clara often longed to go and couldn't afford to. There have been teachers in the Collet family for two hundred years, all of them women until my father. As far as I know I was the first to teach in a state school; though the issue of how to educate for a working life and how to educate the poor, whether in India or in London, were Collet preoccupations from the beginning of the eighteenth century. Joseph Collet wrote home from India in 1717 to describe the school he was setting up 'for the instruction of the Natives':

> Our own free School is a Noble foundation; there are between 30 to 40 Children of both Sexes already provided for, not only with all the Conveniencys of Life but also with an Education to fit them to provide for themselves hereafter. We are about building a handsome Colledge for their Entertainment.

The fact that both Jews and Unitarians were kept out of universities until the last quarter of the nineteenth century meant that families in both groups took trouble to educate girls and women, believing that the family must be the place where education began and might continue, and that women were needed as participants in the process. Money made a difference there too, though, for most of the women in my Jewish family were reared for marriage rather than paid employment until well into the twentieth century, in spite of their education, while Collet women – those at least who did not marry, and there were a fair number of those – have been earning their living for more than two hundred years.

'I like you playing on your Musick,' Samuel Collet wrote to his son Joseph in 1726, 'but remember it is only an amusement and business is what must recommend you to men of sence and the world.' Three years later he wrote to his brother, the other Joseph, now retired and back in England after his years in Madras, 'I have enquired & at last got a Sight of Handells Lessons but they ask me a Guinea for it; it consists of about 96 pages, so I thought it so dear you would hardly care for it but tell me in your next whether you will have it or no.' Samuel grudgingly encouraged one son to bring his harpsichord back with him from Stockholm if it would make him happy, and there is talk of a viol to be given as a present to another son, John, the doctor. Music was important to the Collets even when it interfered with making money and theological debate. John bought Eliza an early nineteenth-century piano – the sort my father occasionally played on the BBC Third Programme in

the 1950s – and John and Eliza's children, Collet and
Sophy, earned at least some of their living as musicians:
as singers, pianists, composers, teachers. Wilfred, Collet's
son and my grandfather, trained the band in Suva and
transcribed the music his father had sent him for the
third and fourth cornets in a band that was obliged to
play on two nights running, for the admiral's ball as well
as the governor's. Wilfred himself played the organ and
the clarinet – instruments my father never had much
time for. It was his beloved aunt Edith who started him
on the piano and the violin. If music spelled some sort
of harmony and pleasure in the family, it also brought
discord: business versus amusement, careers versus art,
professionals versus amateurs. By the twentieth century
there were Salaman musicians too. My mother's younger
sister Esther has been a singer and a teacher of singers,

and there have been professional as well as good amateur musicians among my grandfather's children and
grandchildren. Perhaps only Clara and I have been hap-
pier listening to music than playing it.

There are other themes that persist in the history of
my families as they must in many others. Trade and imper-
ial obligations took members of both families all over
Europe, the Empire, the colonies, and to the Far East
and India especially. Joseph Collet wrote home from
Madras to his four daughters, sending them silks and
jewels and advising them to read the Bible. He wrote
most often to his favourite and oldest daughter, Elizabeth,
telling her in one letter that he was sending her 'a black
Girl named Flora. I bought her in this place and send

her a present to your Self. She talks English and can work a little.' He even went so far as to remind his daughter to 'consider her as your Slave, and consequently that you may employ or dispose of her as you please'. He meant, I think, that Flora might be sold in England for profit. There is no record of what happened to her.

The ostrich feather trade, which made the Salaman family rich in the nineteenth century, had offices in Paris, New York, Port Elizabeth and Cape Town by the end of the century. Young men from both families took off to make their fortunes in Australia and New Zealand from the 1830s onwards and settled there. There are bays and lakes in both countries as well as mountains and high passes through them, and humbler 'knolls', named after some of them. India recurred as a lure and a passion for generations of Collets, and two of my own three children have married Parsees, a brother and sister from Bombay, producing between them four children to delight the eye and heart of their grandmother and to further confuse and enrich the genetic pool my mother so casually took credit for.

The names are gone for the most part: there were too many girls on both sides. 'Collet', at least, persists in my part of the family only as a piously bestowed middle name, though 'Samuel' and 'Joseph' have survived as first names, if inadvertently, to commemorate those old traders and Dissenters rather than the Jews you might have expected to answer to them. Happily, my grandchildren go to schools where their so-called 'mixed-race' inheritance is the norm rather than the exception. One or two of them are good at fractions and enjoy expressing themselves in quarters and eighths. But the 'us' and 'them' of Home Secretaries and census-gatherers are merged now, as we are. A new generation makes its own enquiries about family, belonging, happiness. Only Joseph, the oldest of my six grandchildren, knew my father, and he is proud of the music connection. He resembles the most endearing of his forebears in wanting to play his guitar more than anything else, and is occasionally reminded, as they were, that it is work that makes the world go round. He managed not long ago to fit himself into my father's tails and to wear them with panache for his band's latest gig.

Happiness

My father expected us to think of ourselves as agnostics and not atheists. This was to encourage politeness about other people and their passions, I think, rather than to prepare us for a surprise call from the Almighty. It was also, I dare say, a legacy of his Unitarian background, if not upbringing. My mother had her own personal god, on the other hand, who kept a kindly and unhusbandly eye on her thoughts and behaviour at all times, though she could never explain to us how he managed to do so while attending to his other cares. I offered a version of this information to the undertaker when my father died. Bright as a button, in dusky pink and glittering spectacles, she assured us that when it came to funeral sermons her firm could 'go as low as you like'. But my sisters and I decided against even that and did instead as our father had asked us to in his will. There was no mention of God at his funeral – though that's not true, because we played a tape of Bach's 'Erbarme dich, mein Gott', more for our sakes than his – and his three daughters spoke about three of the things that were important to him: music, France and the past.

For six months before he died he sat up in bed in three different hospitals, transparently thin, angry as I had never known him, and refusing all comforts or consolation, music, books, food, drink, visits home. He had had a charmingly crooked smile, and proffered a wintry imitation of it now at the news that three more great-grandchildren were currently gestating, as if he didn't expect, or didn't want, to be there when they arrived; and he wasn't. He was often silent during those months, though sometimes he would break into his old topics: detailed family histories of people he'd known as a child, full of second wives and mistresses, all of them living in Maidenhead or Newbury, it seemed to me; the story of Yugoslavia and its warring parts and factions going pretty well as far back as the Middle Ages, or the horrors of contemporary pronunciation: draw*r*ing, light*b*olb and Muni*ch,* when it should – of course – be either München or Muni*ck.* A nurse asked me to give him a shower on one visit, and when I suggested that he might prefer to wash his own parts, he contemplated them sadly and remarked, 'I have the very distinct impression that they've become smaller recently': not a proposition to which I felt qualified to respond. His two-volume Pléiade edition of Ronsard lay on the hospital locker by his bed, a hideous carton of sputum beside it.

I remember his last visit to my house, on a freezing February day, an unexpected and battered brown trilby askew on his wild grey hair as a gesture intended to withstand the cold. He had been forced by my mother and her hunger for company to come to London when he should have been in bed. A week before that he had sat on his own at a magically dramatised performance, produced by his son-in-law, of the *St Matthew Passion* in a church, and refused a lift, even to the station. He let me wait for him in my car, though, the next day, as he tried on new glasses at the optician's, and I remember watching him through the shop window, as he flirted a bit with the girl behind the desk, his eyes made bluer by the thicker lens. But age and illness suddenly brought exasperation, impatience, shrinkage. My mother maddened him as she sat by his hospital bed – perhaps we all did – yet he expected frequent visits from us and always thanked us politely for coming, with apologies for complicating our lives. Every now and then an ancient and hitherto stagnant resentment of my mother boiled up and over and he blamed her, a spoiled 'princess', for her rich, Jewish family's mistrust of him: a lifetime's self-control finally spent, gone, like perished elastic. His fine curved nose became a small yellow beak as he lay dying. My mother missed him sorely.

He left more at his death than he can have anticipated. There was not much money, but a house that had multiplied at least three hundred times in value since he bought it from a friend for the £1,000 his father left him for this purpose (a sum which neither grew nor shrank as it was exchanged for progressively smaller houses over the early years of his marriage). There was a large library of books and music scores, most of it in languages other than English and damp with mildew, and a set of tails with accompanying starched shirts and piqué waistcoats, all too narrow, it turns out, for most of his descendants. There were a few letters too, and I shall come to them; and among the clarinets, bassoon, violins and viola, the metronomes and the tottering piles of music on his two grand pianos (one of them fitted with weighted keys for morning scales and arpeggios), we found some old cheques from the BBC, long-since invalid.

He also left at least thirty notebooks filled with what amounts to a whole book about Liszt's piano music, some chapters on Chopin, Berlioz and Busoni and plans for others on Schubert and Alkan. The writing is clear and uncluttered, written on alternate lines of alternate pages, with hardly any crossings-out, though there are passages so technical and detailed that only a few people (the very ones in a position to disagree with him, I suppose) would want to read it. Yet he is strangely concerned with the views of 'the public, both in its more and in its less intelligent sections' – strangely, because he gives no sense of having met or even visualised such *sections*, though he is absolutely sure that none of them has got it right. Liszt's uncertain reputation stood for him as an example of the public's sheeplike adherence to 'good taste', and he traces contemptuously what he saw as *their* 'contempt for the falsity, the meretriciousness and the bombast of Liszt's music' to the 'Brahms, Joachim and Clara Schumann circle', which had set attitudes in train that persisted through several generations, so that 'in musical circles it was considered a hallmark of rectitude and the highest standards of taste' to express contempt for Liszt. There is 'something deeply ambiguous about Liszt's music as about his personality,' my father wrote, and 'ambivalence and ambiguity excite distrust'. There are, in addition, references to 'people with a casual knowledge of ' some subject or other – not a group he had much time for – as well as to 'most musicians' and even to 'most people', another generally misguided lot, which may possibly have included his family and friends.

The notebooks also contain his translations of the libretto of Berlioz's opera *Béatrice et Bénédict*, and of Goethe's words that inspired Liszt's *Faust Symphony* ('But what is this that lights the wood up so brightly?'); and then abruptly, in the middle of another such notebook, there are lists of Czech words from the time when he was teaching himself Czech, and several copied-out

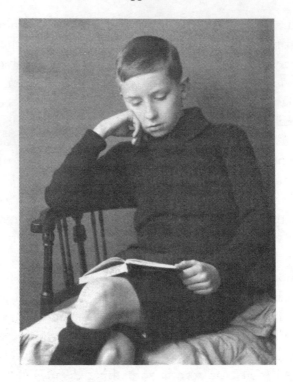

poems and sentences, all meticulously accented. He had been commissioned to write the book on Liszt, but he hated writing it, felt it for years as the most gruelling burden, and he gave up in the end, a whisker away from finishing it.

My father was once a fair-haired, serious and round-faced little boy, who wrote sonnets in French as well as English when he was eleven, some of them to Lord Kitchener. He was by far the youngest of three sons. His oldest brother was twenty years older, while a younger one died after suffering for all of his short life from one of those conditions families kept under their hats, successfully in this case, though his mother wrote to her sister-in-law Carrie, when Jack was about eight or nine, describing his slow progress towards learning to speak and controlling his restlessness. Perhaps they simply didn't know what was wrong with him. My father certainly never knew. Their mother Mary, originally from Adelaide (her family had settled later in Fiji, where she met Wilfred at the beginning of his career in the Colonial Service), died of influenza when my father was five, an out-come that was relayed to him by a well-meaning neighbour he barely knew. I imagine that he was expected not to cry, and certainly didn't. Clara, another of her sisters-in-law, recorded

Mary's death and the medical report on it in her diary, adding, 'she had a beautiful character'. As his father was mostly away, governing swampy outposts of the Empire like British Honduras and British Guiana, my father grew up as an only child and more or less an orphan in the Hampstead house of his aunts and uncle, none of whom had married. Caroline, the eldest, and Edith, the youngest, were teachers at the time, who taught at Camden School for Girls and the North London Collegiate School. Their sister Clara we have met. She was a more worldly person altogether, this civil servant, economist and writer, who often lived elsewhere and on her own. In later years my father sometimes wondered why none of his aunts had married. 'They were not bad-looking, after all,' he would mutter worriedly. His uncle Harold, golfer and authority on water softening, and also not bad-looking, was assumed to have chosen his bachelor state.

My father saw very little of his father, who wrote to him regularly, however, on handsome ivory-coloured writing paper, addressing him as Phoebus Apollo and signing off as Zeus. From my father's point of view, this knight of the realm in his gold braid and cocked hat (or, alternatively, white ducks) seems often to have been an obstacle to his hopes and ambitions and possibly too devoted to his own. He allowed his son to go to Bedales when he was twelve or so and recovering from appendicitis with complications, but he drew the line later when this same son announced that he wanted to be a pianist. Perhaps this was because his own father had resisted a career in the law or the Civil Service as a young man in favour of a musical career, and had in fact had a hard time of it supporting his large family on what he earned as a singer in the chorus at Covent Garden. At sixteen my father began a history degree at University College London, completing it with a first in record time in order to earn the right to read music at Cambridge after that, where he studied with the Mephistophelian Edward Dent.

Pictures of my father as a child, and letters written to him and by him, suggest a preternaturally obliging little boy and a learner who had learned to be eternally grateful to the relations who had taken him in. He wrote obediently and often to his father, and later, when he was at boarding school, more cheerfully and openly to

his favourite aunt, Edith, whom he called Athene. In one letter, he explained his theory of money to her:

I have thought out a scheme for people doing without money. People are always to receive enough to keep them <u>vegitating</u> (to <u>vegitate</u> they needn't work); but to have luxuries and <u>live</u>, they must work. The right to have more than just enough to keep body and soul together, is the payment of labour, confirmation of the right is a certificate of work. The value of the certificate varies according to the amount of work performed, and the certificates are used accordingly. The state issues the certificate.

Not an original scheme, perhaps – though it seems more sensible than his adult conviction that mortgages were immoral – but interesting for its prefiguring at twelve of my father's later horror (or perhaps terror) of money. It was in the same year, 1918, that he and 'Athene' seem to have shared in what must have been a fashionable fondness for the by then defunct Russian Provisional Government and in the hero-worshipping of Kerensky, its leader, who had so recently been the darling of the St Petersburg intelligentsia. In that same year my father taught himself the Russian alphabet and sent his father the names of all the members of the Duma, written in Russian script. 'Athene', meanwhile, sent him an excited description of the gloomy Kerensky himself, speaking in London to a hall full of enthusiasts. 'He looked,' she told her nephew, 'about 100', and she drew his mouth as a letter box, speculating that the Russian language might require mouths to be that shape. In the Second World War my father learned Russian, and it was one of the languages he came to know best.

He met Arthur Salaman and his younger brother Raphael when he was still at Bedales, and he began to spend parts of the school holidays at their home in Barley, near Cambridge, in 1925, the year their mother died. Someone took a photograph of him behaving foolishly on the lawn, and he was remembered playing the piano in the nursery. There had been some mild trouble at Bedales when he cropped up three times in one of those long rolling school photographs, and later when he dressed up as Arthur's aunt and took him out to tea on a Saturday afternoon. Mostly, however, he was sober and hard-working and an excellent passer of exams, even maths ones, which caused more suspicion than admiration at a school which lovingly fostered weaving, sawing logs and milking cows, regarding exams and other forms of competition as the work of the devil.

In the late 1920s, after University College London and three years at Cambridge, he spent a year or so in Berlin studying German and the piano. His father must have given him a small allowance as well as paying the fees of this incipiently perpetual student. His piano teacher in England, Frieda Kindler, a pianist and a pupil of Busoni, married to the writer and composer Bernard Van Dieren, wrote to his father early in 1929 to remind him of his son's talent and of the necessity for exercising a proper sense of responsibility towards it. This must have been an attempt to mollify and secure more financial support from Sir Wilfred, who was becoming impatient for his son to earn a living. Presumably the appeal fell on stony ground, for that was the year when my father returned for the first time to Bedales as a teacher, where he spent at least two years teaching the piano and working with the student orchestra. He complains, in a letter to his father, about the impossibility of controlling his pupils' unruly behaviour at mealtimes, especially when there are girls at his table as well as boys.

He had known my mother slightly for several years, as the older of the two young sisters of his Salaman friends, before he took much notice of her. He was twenty-six and she twenty-two when they began an affair. She was back at home again after three or four years of London independence at the Slade School of Art. She had sent several flustered bulletins from that arena of love to Esther, her newly acquired Russian sister-in-law, who was clearly already an exotic and important figure in her life and later in the whole family's, now that her mother was dead and her father remarried. My mother's passions seem always to have raged simultaneously as well as serially. There was a woman she loved 'in spite of her ugliness', who taught the violin at Bedales and loved another. Then there was her art teacher there, on whom she doted, but who was given to 'mad ravings'. She announces her suicidal desperation at the beginning of one letter, assuring her sister-in-law that her 'heart will litrally biologically bleed', though she admits a little further down that 'I cant concentrate on misery for very long you see'. Later, there was the wily Henry Tonks, who had awarded her a scholarship to the Slade, but was usually involved with one of his models and was, anyway, as my mother put it, 'an octigenarian'. She felt bad about her uncomfortable parrying of attempts made on her virtue by a fellow student at the Slade, whom she thought 'fat and short and unattractive', though she had let him kiss her and was now distraught to find that he expected her to move her easel into his studio and serve his talent rather than he hers.

She remembered my father sixty years later as a 'cathedral' and a 'prodigy', with his light blue eyes, dark hair and romantic good looks; but she was never sure that she had been in love with him, and she remained for ever 'young for her age', as far as he was concerned, well into her eighties. In a letter written three years after their marriage and also to Esther, my father ungallantly wrote of his wife that she

has undoubtedly a difficult character from some points of view, mostly due in my opinion to her

upbringing having been badly mismanaged. Her
two greatest difficulties are a serious tendency to
perpetual worry about all kinds of things, and an
introspective tendency to indecision.

Ungallant, and with more than a grain of truth, of course,
but – in the way of marital admissions – at least as much
a description of him as of her.

Suddenly, however, she was pregnant, and the two of
them were on the boat train to Paris and a *mairie* wedding, only to find it was a false alarm. I was actually
born in 1932, nearly a year after they married. The wit-
nesses (the marriage took place in the British Consulate
in Paris, in fact) were two old friends. One famously
disappeared during the Second World War and was never
seen or heard of again, though ritually asked after year
in, year out, by all his old schoolfriends, for there were
reported sightings in South America, which came to
nothing. The other witness, the girl my mother knew
from school, was the one who ran away with my father
about four years later, though the adventure was swiftly
aborted and the pair somehow 'brought home'.

My father's letters to his aunts and uncle announcing
his marriage give little away. Neither family welcomed
the news. His aunt Clara kept the sour draft of the brief
letter she wrote him among her papers:

I do not doubt your joint judgment in not dawdling
over it, and especially staying in Paris for the wedding, although the Salamans at home may feel
cheated out of a little exciting bustle . . . May your
dreams all come true although it will need a lot of
hard work.

This manages to be superior on several fronts, most obviously about the Salamans, who she likes to imagine as frustrated in their silly desire for fuss and ritual. She made it quite clear to my mother that she thought her 'empty-headed' and 'shallow' and continued to hope, in vain, for an improvement in her spelling. Clara also managed to suggest that Edith, my father's favourite aunt, would find the news so unsettling that she, Clara, was considering keeping it from her, in the interests of her health and peace of mind.

It was perverse of my parents to marry each other. I think of them as egged on by family disapproval, by anxiety about her pregnancy, and by their being at that moment in their lives when decisions were expected and a move of some sort towards adulthood became mandatory. Perhaps it was important, too, that they both thought of themselves as artists, and different in that respect from their families. My grandfather was very fond of his older daughter, in spite of her spelling and other failings, and he was keen for her to marry a Jew. In addition, he reckoned at once that this son-in-law would find it hard to make a living, had no courage or aptitude for investment, and though handsome and clever was not going to keep his daughter in the style to which she had been accustomed and would surely expect thereafter.

He was quite wrong, as it happens, on that front, since my mother took like a duck to water to having rather little money, a small house and no servants. To the day she died she regarded anyone who offered to help her (paid or unpaid) as an interference, likely to impose a quite unnecessary and even reprehensible order and cleanliness on her perfectly acceptable mess. She was not a natural housewife, to put it mildly, but the fact is that she enjoyed her various uncomfortable homes over the years and even in some ways enjoyed looking after her husband and children. Her diaries spell out her pleasure in all this, conveyed with a humorous awareness that she was thought by most people to fall rather far short as a family provider. She felt reproved by her neighbours' gardening prowess, for instance, and wrote of some new arrivals, 'What wouldn't it feel like if just for once we had some slow coaches next door?' 'Trying' was what mattered in her view, an approach to life instilled by Bedales, where 'marks for effort' could so far exceed those for achievement as to upset all conventional views of satisfactory activity of any kind. I used regularly to get a D1 for the violin, for instance, when I was at Bedales: the 1 was for effort and the top mark. The D was for where it had got me. Of the morning before a trip to Paris, my mother wrote in her diary, 'Got up at five thirty and went straight downstairs to re-iron B's trousers, which the previous night I had ironed two inches out of the true.' I think, though, that my grandfather sensed something more than a likely absence of money and comfort, or even of compatibility, in all this. He thought that my father was in some vital sense not the marrying sort.

And he probably wasn't. It is strange and sad to think of one's arrival in the world as coterminous with, if not the cause of, someone else's fate being sealed for ever. If it was, it was because he decided it was; and that was perverse too. Of course, many children, especially first ones, must have been perceived in that light, if only momentarily, and it is the energetic egotism of young children that protects them from the full implications of this. Despite his desultory bid for freedom four years later (and I admit that I have difficulty imagining it as other than desultory), my father seems always to have insisted that he would stay married to my mother, even were she to want the marriage to end. Habits of obedience, of being, and of being thought, a good boy, died hard. There were jobs he did and habits he developed as proof of this: washing and drying up, with a dishcloth permanently draped over his shoulder like a Brahmin's, and constantly checking that the boiler was alight. But he had no interest in household matters, let alone in initiating family activities or occasions. He enjoyed the thought of family as one kind of window on the past. He kept the letters written to his grandfather by Karl Marx in his sock drawer, his own Fort Knox; and there were those who thought that if ever the letters were bequeathed to a library the drawer – and perhaps the socks – should go as well. I'm not sure that the family he had helped to create had as much appeal for him as the one he had grown up in, though he loved us, I think, in his way.

My parents settled in Paris in 1932, and at the end of that year I was born, and they rearranged their small flat in the Rue de la Tombe Issoire to accommodate a baby, while also putting up occasional friends who were passing through. My mother wrote letters to her husband's aunt Edith, filled with drawings of me, and confessing to her impatience with housework and her interest in inventing puddings. She sounds happy. There was, in fact, a *femme de ménage* and it may have been she who took me for walks while my newly married parents pursued their studies. She was making her prints and etchings and engravings in the studio of Stanley William Hayter, and he was working with his piano teacher, Isidore Philipp. They went back to England from time to time, and then in the early summer of 1934 my father gave two Wigmore Hall recitals in London. Financially, these did not break even, and there were one or two cruel reviews among the encouraging ones. Several congratulated him on his playing while reviling his choice of pieces by Busoni, Van Dieren and Liszt. The most interesting review was written by the composer Constant Lambert, who praised him for 'remarkable technical ability' and intelligence, while finding his playing introvert and constrained in ways that were possibly all too well suited to one or two of the pieces

he was tackling. He also wrote tellingly that my father 'could well allow himself a touch of bravura and flamboyance', and I imagine my father rather relishing that judgement. There are no signs that this experience particularly worried or upset him. He was philosophical about it taking a lifetime to perfect technique, and was always grandly impervious to criticism of his programme choices.

My mother came back to London at the end of 1935 to give birth to her second daughter, and my father and I followed. They bought their first house, on North Hill in Highgate, and a year or so after that my father made his one and only bid for freedom, but was back within a week, I believe. It may have been a chance to get back to France. His career as a pianist began to take off in a small way. I remember there were concerts in Birmingham and Belfast; and when paying my second or third visit some years later to the film in which Cornel Wilde played Chopin to Merle Oberon's George Sand – and travelling across Europe on a tour of sell-out concerts was conveyed by a collage of posters spattered with his consumptive nosebleeds – I wondered how my father would have fared if his engagements had taken him further afield. One of his more promising concerts had to be cancelled when he broke his thumb. Not long after that, late in 1938, he became so convinced that a second world war was inevitable that he moved the family to another £1,000 house next to the station in Petersfield in Hampshire and not far from a rest home for exhausted circus lions. Our nights were occasionally disturbed between trains by the sound of the lions' tragic senescent yawns, and my father, who was clearly sympathetic to their plight, became adept at imitating them. He returned to Bedales and taught there throughout the war, and he could not always resist telling us about his dottier pupils. One girl would idly wonder during lessons whether playing the piano wouldn't be much easier if God had given her enough fingers to cover every key of the piano. All very well, she mused, but hardly an inducement to anyone planning to knit gloves for her.

I have the sense that the war was quite a good time for my parents. They both had friends at Bedales and in Petersfield. The house was usually full of lodgers, evacuees, refugees, old friends; and their third daughter was born in 1941. My father joined the Home Guard, taking offhand care of what I think of as their only gun and becoming the platoon's radio operator. As well as learning Russian with Dum Dum, an ancient lady from St Petersburg, who sometimes took us mushrooming and believed that there was only one kind of fungus that was poisonous (a conviction that has stayed with me rather uselessly, since I can't remember which it was), my father read widely on military strategy, subscribed to *France Libre* and listened obsessively to the wireless. He often played the Sunday Voluntary at school, and when he did he was not inclined to pander to adolescent tastes. One evening he played all the Goldberg Variations for what seemed like several hours to the assembled school population, which included an oldest daughter of thirteen, who was currently asserting – with surly resolve – her opposition to all art, culture and learning, and who was humiliated to be caught out like this while in the company of her raffish friends. I delighted in what I thought of (with justification, and the encouragement of both my parents) as my 'ordinariness', and I shivered with

embarrassment at my father's intransigent fastidiousness and highbrow tastes.

My mother, meanwhile, was often in love, with our next-door neighbour and with the beautiful Italian who taught me the fiddle. I averted my gaze from that too. She also did some teaching of printmaking and lettering at the local boys' school. I can summon up one of those all-purpose metonymic memories of her to this day, with her hairpins held between her teeth as she coiled up her long fair hair in what seemed a perpetual and fruitless attempt to keep it and everything else under control.

At the end of the war, my father got a job at the BBC, producing performances of French operas for the Third Programme, working with French singers and conductors and teaching English singers to sing in French. This must have been a good time for him, though I remember that, like all other BBC employees, he grumbled about 'the Corporation' and suffered the particular BBC malaise that Orwell translated with such ease into the totalitarian horrors of *Nineteen Eighty-four*. Music at the BBC was managed by William Glock, an old friend of my father's from Cambridge. From the vantage point of 2003 those seem golden days, and they were, but there were those who looked askance at all the contemporary music that was suddenly filling the radio airwaves, a lot of it composed by Glock's friends, and there were articles in the newspapers about the nepotism and the élitism of all this, given the BBC's mission to educate everybody. There was no talk in those days of 'dumbing down'. My father, however, was in his element, producing operas by Lully and Gluck and Rameau and Berlioz; and he was broadcasting himself: playing work by Szymanowski and by French composers – Alkan, Satie, Fauré, Debussy, Ravel – but playing older music as well, sometimes on the harpsichord or on early nineteenth-century pianos. Occasionally, I turned the pages of his music for him, anxious not to miss a repeat and get it wrong, and occasionally I slipped up and watched the irritation flit across his face like bad weather.

Once or twice he took me to concerts of contemporary music so difficult that pieces were played twice – to my consternation – in order that the audience got the joke or the point. But he didn't stay long at the BBC, three or four years at most. It was as if it was all too good to be true, and therefore somehow not to be borne; but perhaps he also felt compelled to have one last shot at becoming the pianist he had set out to be. There were more Wigmore Hall recitals, with unfashionable programmes, luxuriantly 'modern' for the most part, which got mixed reviews. There were three children now, and though my mother's father helped to pay for our schooling, and though we lived on very little, the money must have dried up altogether by the early fifties. My father became a part-time teacher at Harrow School and a year or two later a professor of piano at a London music college.

What happens to promise? My father didn't fall to bits or drink or lose his memory. Far from it. Until those last six months he got up early to practise the piano every single day for several hours. I was so used as a child to his hours of early morning practice that I could hear it and yet believe myself to be in a silent, empty house. For years he worked hard and uncomplainingly as a teacher, and clearly enjoyed some of it. He wrote articles and chapters about music for his friends' books and journals, and was active in the Liszt Society. He knew London well, especially the City, and loved showing old churches and neglected bits of it to visitors. In the fifties and sixties he often worked in the British Museum Reading Room, where he learned to do a recognisable counter-tenor imitation of Angus Wilson on the telephone, presiding at the library's central desk. When his daughters married he accepted his sons-in-law with imperfect grace, perhaps, but he made no serious objections.

He travelled to France or Germany or Czechoslovakia
every year until he was at least eighty, and in his odd
and rather unkempt way remained tall and slim and
young-looking, no doubt due to the exercises he performed each day on instructions from a Colonel Muehler,
whose book he delighted in, with its demonstration pictures of the naked, moustachioed author and its list of
what might be cured by his regime: imbecility and melan-
cholia as well as backache, I remember. He continued to
read (or rather reread) in each of the six languages he
knew well: *Faust* and *Wilhelm Meister* or Heine's poems
during his scales and arpeggios – always washed down
by his first and enormous mug of black unsugared tea;
Dante when he was stropping his cut-throat razor before

his morning shave; La Fontaine or Victor Hugo or André Gide later in the day, and the poems of Lermontov or Blok in Russian in the evenings. He read poetry and essays, for the most part, hardly ever novels, though he seems to have read almost all nineteenth-century novels in his youth; and he never went to films or plays or watched television, except at the end of his life, the news on Channel 4. He had learned several languages entirely through reading in them, believing that you got a better class of language that way, so there were books by his bed in Polish and modern Greek, which he never really mastered, although he could read in them. Welsh and Hungarian had defeated him, he used to say, though he had tried to learn both, and he liked to remind you that they had defeated quite a lot of other people too.

At some point he had stuck, though, lost heart or appetite, and not just because of age. He stopped reading new things, and his phenomenal memory began to feed on itself, ceasing to mop up thoughts and impressions, producing no new deposits for itself. His reading of newspapers meant that he was up to date with events in the world, but he read almost no new writing. In old age he was given to asking potential grandsons-in-law or other new acquaintances whether they knew (or rather 'had') German and shaking his head mournfully – 'pity, pity' – when they confessed that they didn't, rather as Carlyle might have done had he not been reminded by his old friend Francis Jeffrey that it wouldn't do to 'treat the whole Earth not yet Germanized as a "parcel of blockheads"'. My father needed a friend like that. Perhaps his gifts atrophied from disappointment and disuse, though that isn't the whole story. He seemed positively to welcome pretexts for escape from struggle, ambition, hope, and I once entertained for five minutes or so the outrageous thought that my father was naturally lazy and wanted an easy life. He was never short of people to talk to; rather, he became less and less able (or willing) to insert what he knew and wanted to say into conversations he had not initiated and was not in control of. He could fall asleep instantly, as his interlocutor was speaking, and often did. I learned to speak fast in order to circumvent this habit of his, watching beadily as his eyes began to close and his head slumped back against the headrest of his armchair; and in adolescence I knew, for instance, that requests for money to go to London were more likely to be frustrated by his intense boredom at hearing me out than by outright refusal. He once announced a scheme to fine me a halfpenny for every 'sort of' I uttered; but inertia predictably defeated both pedantry and greed, and I don't remember that I handed over more than a penny or two.

His knowledge remained, but it petrified, and all those languages, all that fluency and precision of speech, availed him not at all when he found himself outside what might be thought of as some variant of the tutorial relation. His vast range of reference, people he had known and known about, in Paris or Brno or L'vov (the last two meticulously and correctly pronounced), all this became stranded, cut off from the mainland. Perhaps he longed – and his daughters longed for it for him – for a world of *semblables*, of equals. Perhaps, I used to think, he'd have been happy as an unmarried don in a small Cambridge college, intimate only with the woman who made his bed, though ready to light up for an admiring student. Then I think of Gibbon recalling the Oxford fellows of his youth: 'From the toil of reading, or thinking, or writing, they had absolved their conscience.' Perhaps he would have liked that, found it a relief. Or perhaps he missed the excitement, the hint of decadence, he'd known as a student and in Berlin and then in the world of the Van Dierens and London music.

My father let his life be shaped by two perverse decisions, whose consequences he obstinately allowed to be inescapable. The first was to become a concert pianist, a virtuoso, as he called it (rather surprisingly, I think) in his youth: for he not only lacked the 'bravura and flamboyance' Constant Lambert had recommended, he heartily disapproved of such qualities, especially in pianists. In that article which movingly explains his admiration for the pianist Vlado Perlemuter, and for what he thought of as a peculiarly French combination of musical range and subtlety of technique in Perlemuter's playing, my father wrote:

If his virtuosity may seem to dazzle less than the virtuosity of a Horowitz, this is surely simply that its aim is never in the first place to dazzle. He may sometimes make an unusual choice of *tempo*, but it is never dictated by any but musical considerations; some of the Chopin *Preludes* and *Studies* were in fact taken at unusually moderate *tempi*, with a great gain in musical expressiveness. Perlemuter's technique would have obviously permitted him to take them at any speed that he thought fit. No doubt only a real virtuoso can know just how to put virtuosity in its right place.

Despite his total lack of anything approaching showmanship, my father enjoyed playing in public, and it always seemed to me that he played with an evident determination to 'explain' the music he was playing and to hear its composer's purpose and structure, rather than setting out to impress technically, something I believe he could easily have done, in fact. He knew that this kind of care and inwardness in a pianist was unfashionable, but he stuck to his guns. I don't believe that he ever regretted working so hard to be a pianist or felt much surprise that his successes had been as limited as they were.

The second decision – to marry and father children, girls in his case – is harder still to be sure about. He may not have been cut out for bravura performance or for paternity, but he did not complain or appear to be sorry for himself, or give signs of longing for other things – though occasional bursts of temper gave hints of an unruly inner life that was not ordinarily visible, and he harboured lifelong grudges (mostly unspoken) against his father and his father-in-law, as if they stood for some rule or order he felt compelled to obey and resented.

A letter he wrote when he was twenty-nine, in 1935, has recently come to light. My mother was pregnant with the older of my two younger sisters. My father was writing to the sister-in-law who had fielded my mother's letters when they were full of her incipient love affairs at the Slade, and who kept some of these letters and appears to have answered them too. This Aunt Esther (I have another one, who is my mother's sister) was born in 1900 in Zhitomir in the Ukraine and had, when she was eighteen, made her way from there to Palestine, eventually getting her whole family out during the pogroms of 1920. Later, she studied as a physicist with

Einstein in Germany, who sent her to Cambridge and
the Cavendish Laboratory there. She met and married
my mother's oldest brother (another scientist), had four
children, gave up physics and eventually wrote several
novels and two wonderful books about the uses of
memory in literature.

My parents' letters to her must have held something
of her own early years in England, and perhaps that is
why she kept them. This letter from my father is a
spectacularly long one for him to have written (his letters were usually terse to a fault): ten foolscap sides
(and still some final pages are missing), meticulously
handwritten, perhaps even a fair copy of a rough draft.
It is a surprising letter to discover so long after it was

written, and something of a revelation: not only for *what* it reveals, but for its profound self-absorption and its clarity and display of openness. It is a letter asking for help, understanding and discretion, which sets out its author's dilemma as if in a court of law. There are headings and subheadings, and the whole thing is punctuated by warnings and instructions about how it is to be read.

It starts by explaining why he and my mother have decided to stay in France after all (though this was revoked soon afterwards, and in fact they came back to England for good). This soon-to-be-reversed decision is defended in terms of his work, his love of France, his sense that a life of playing and writing about music and teaching could be managed in Paris ('the French Paris not the cosmopolitan' one), as he insists (unconvincingly) that it couldn't in London. The letter maps a cerebral and abstract landscape of splittings and dualities: France versus England; acquiring technical virtuosity as a pianist versus teaching and writing; doing one's 'best work' and studying on the one hand, a career on the other; quality or quantity. There is always some contest implied as well between ambition and caution, the short term rather than the long, and so on. And the solution to these oppositions is always an attempt somehow to accommodate 'both', in ways which seek to deny the very polarities he has so insistently set up. He worries about sounding precious or dishonest or about seeming to oversimplify the position; and eventually he reaches the second of his themes, the 'future success and happiness of our married life'. The motifs of doubleness increase exponentially at this point.

Everything he has to say about his marriage is offered

as reinforcement for their staying in France rather than returning to England. In this sense, it is a wilful letter and even a slyly advocatory one. He reminds his sister-in-law of the doubts expressed by almost everyone about the marriage. He, though, is inclined to see the difficulties they are currently having as no more than any young married couple might experience, but – and at this point he branches into *three* sets of reasons for their difficulties – there are some special circumstances. One of these is that he is earning nothing and living on the last of his father's allowance. This is a strain (for him). There is his wife's 'difficult character', and I have already quoted what he had to say about that. Finally, there is, as he puts it, his

> undoubtedly unusual sexual temperament, all the more peculiar in its abnormality perhaps, from the fact that in some ways – in most indeed – it is quite ordinary. From a very early age, I have had a strong need and desire for emotional – for strongly emotional friendships with men, and my make-up undoubtedly contains quite a strong dose of what is rather loosely called homosexuality. On the other hand my feelings towards R are entirely those of a normal heterosexual man, and lacking neither in spontaneity nor in intensity from an erotic point of view.

This, he admits, is 'the most serious question of all', and five points flow from it. He wants to come clean with his sister-in-law, as he already has with his wife and had indeed before they were married. He thinks of himself as bisexual, and is looking for some midway point, some solution: a compromise between exercising 'self-discipline as best I can' and the positive acknowledgement of his homosexuality. If it is driven underground it would become 'a real menace to my married happiness, and my spiritual sanity'. He assures his sister-in-law that he has 'never "gone the whole hog"', and that whenever he has come close to doing so he has drawn back, sensing that this isn't what he wants. He explains:

> I have quite frequently felt towards men feelings of an unquestionably erotic character, but I have felt always (and I think it is an instinctive, not a moral reaction) that there would be something essentially false and unsatisfying in any attempt to put my relations with a man I was fond of on a physical sexual basis; and the greater my affection for the man the more the sexual relationship would be misplaced. I could only really regard such a sexual relationship as possible with a man for whom I had no affection and no respect, and then only as the most miserable of makeshifts, designed to procure the illusion of filling up the gap caused by the absence of the emotional and affective male relationship that I need and desire.

He has 'always felt that homosexuality is something that is in itself neither healthy nor diseased, but having potentialities of being both; but for various rather obscure reasons, the conditions of a "healthy homosexuality" are <u>extraordinarily</u> difficult to create'. The letter ends with a demonstration of what he means: an account of his passionate feelings for a Frenchman, a friend of them both (he was to be my younger sister's godfather, in later years, and my mother 'adored' him to the day she died), who had at first listened to but then angrily repudiated my father's idiosyncratic offer of a lopsided friendship, which would recognise his emotional needs without reciprocating their expression (a diagrammatic version of things that determinedly resists translation into any entirely recognisable reality). There had been a long and painful *froideur*, and then at exactly the moment when reconciliation seemed imminent, the Frenchman had sent my parents a note: 'My very dear friends, don't expect me tomorrow; this morning my father fell from the roof of Ste. Geneviève and was killed outright.'

My father's introspection is even more surprising to me than the innocence or naivety of the letter and its relentless forensic drive. I never for a moment, during more than sixty years of knowing my father, got the least glimpse of this capacity for introspection. Nor did he ever mention any aspect of his emotional or sexual life to me or, I think, to my sisters, though he gratefully acknowledged her reference to his homosexuality when my youngest sister brought the subject up at the very end of his life. On the one occasion when, as an adult, I confessed to him that I was unhappy, he laughed complicitously and quoted something world-weary from Balzac. And although he so resoundingly overturns my expectations in this letter, he could also be said to write about his feelings as if he were inventing a genre and had never heard of other people feeling like this, as if there were no literature, no language for investigating such states of mind and being. He is locked into the movement of his own desires and desolation to the point where other people are there only to hear and learn, and his letter organises them with impatient asperity into doing so. He brooks no wonderings from the reader, no scepticism, no idle thoughts about his just possibly protesting too much. Then I wonder what he could have read in 1935 or earlier that might have echoed what he was feeling, or informed him about it, even furnished a language? The letter gives no clues. He was not much interested in psychoanalysis, and a good deal of what was written about sex was, I imagine, concerned with precisely those notions and proofs of normality which he incorporates into his account of his own sexual nature, and which compelled him to marry and stay married, whatever happened. Yet there is an unspoken sense that he has permission to think and talk like this about his sexual feelings, and perhaps that is thanks to Freud.

My father spent most of his life among women, and it is significant that this letter was addressed to a woman. But I think he was most at ease, not among men, but in the romantic and idealised male company his reading offered him: European, mostly nineteenth-century, fenced off from the local and domestic English world of his own life, from the female, the family, the modern and even, perhaps, from the American. I have the sense that Anglo-American culture seemed to him to be lit by too glaring and simplifying a light, with too much emphasis on the shared and the social. Instead, there is a detectable presence in much of his reading of the lonely, contemplative, even exiled, hero, living out the drama of his destiny and his sacrifices in his head: Lermontov's *A Hero of Our Time*, among others. This hero is never contemporary and rarely English. My father returned throughout his life to André Gide's essays and novels and journals – Gide's being both married and homosexual may well have been an attraction – and he enjoyed reading

Baudelaire and Rimbaud. He had read Proust in his youth, but Proust was not one of the writers to whom he returned. I think he was too interested in high society for my father. I suppose he may have read Havelock Ellis, though that is hard to imagine. It is harder still to think of him warming to the English dandies and aesthetes of the thirties or to writers like John Lehmann or Stephen Spender or to Bloomsbury generally, though he admired the early Auden. He actively disliked the music of Stravinsky and later of Benjamin Britten, though he was interested in Peter Warlock and fascinated by Edward Dent. The possible sexual ambiguities of Liszt and Busoni and Van Dieren intrigued him, however. If he had an active homosexual life, I doubt that it brought with it much in the way of a social life, let alone the kind of romantic friendship he longed for, imagined for himself and claimed occasionally to have experienced, in that letter of 1935.

He was not made for drama, and it seems entirely in character that Goethe's *Faust, Part II*, which is almost never staged, should have been his favourite play. In addition, I think of him as given to puncturing and laying bare anything that seemed to him fanciful, overheated, unreasonable, conceited. Yet one friend disappeared into the ether and his French friend's father leapt from the roof of a church, while the same friend's unpopular brother was shot at the end of the Second World War as a collaborator. My father had a wracked expression for contemplating such events and a way of pursing his lips to suggest grim resignation to their occurrence, but I am not at all certain that he was deeply touched by them. For years I have almost hoped to discover that he was one of the Cambridge spies: he was there a bit early, it is true, though several old friends of his were stalwart members of the Communist Party (he had himself been drawn to communism as an adolescent) and one, who later taught in Princeton and had worked with Robert J. Oppenheimer at Los Alamos during the war, lost his job during the McCarthy period. My father's frequent visits to Czechoslovakia and occasionally to East Germany from the 1960s to the 1980s, and his learning of Russian and Czech and Polish, gave some substance to such fantasies. But I am virtually certain that fantasies are what they were. He had a terror of being in the wrong and of impulsiveness, and his politics were never radical enough even for me, let alone for treason.

This unworldly man, whom an old friend of mine remembers for his 'dry humour and distant pleasantries', believed above all in realism and moderation. He insisted that we think of ourselves as 'middle middle-class', regarding any claim on my mother's side of the family to being 'upper middle-class' as pretentious and unwarranted. He always voted for the Liberal Party, even at its lowest ebb, and he liked, wryly, to think of himself as an Asquithian Liberal, if only to demonstrate his resistance to what he considered the demagogy and fraudulence of Lloyd George. But in the end, politics was a spectacle that didn't involve him. He could tell you anything you wanted to know about most Members of Parliament and government ministers, except what they were up to politically or what they believed they were up to.

In his remote and preoccupied way he was interested in his daughters and encouraging to us. Yet my most vivid memories are of his realistic assessments of me. He was an arch-deflater. One letter to his father-in-law includes the sentence 'it is by no means certain that Jane

is a girl who should go to a university', as if universities might need protection from such a person. These
doubts registered my adolescent philistinism, I expect,
and they probably propelled me into going to one. I
know that my grandfather was occasionally moved to
defend me against my father's withering prognoses,
pointing out that I didn't look so bad and had made
quite a fist of sorting out his scientific offprints or of
discussing *Macbeth* with him. My father worried about
our giving ourselves airs and about all sorts of things
going to our heads. When once or twice I performed
in some dramatic or musical production at school, he
was quick to point out just how modest my talents were

and to suggest that I might benefit, as he once put it, from 'a steadier and less stimulating environment'. This was offered as his reason for removing me from Bedales when I was sixteen and sending me to the local girls' school, close to where we lived outside London, though it is just as likely that he was running out of money (my 'free' place didn't cover everything). I took it badly, never quite forgave him for the 'realistic' account of my few strengths and many weaknesses that he proceeded enthusiastically to parade before my new headmistress. These began with the words, I remember, 'She's not much good at . . .' I can't, fortunately, remember all of what followed. Perhaps I decided not to listen.

When finally I was about to follow a glamorous older friend to Cambridge, I was reminded that I should not expect to do as well as she had, since I couldn't hold a candle to her in either looks or brains. I would simply have to work very much harder than she had. At the time I thought this behaviour due to his dislike of swank, and I privately approved of what I took to be a proper truthfulness and austerity, though I always longed for something else, of course. He was incapable of boasting about himself and therefore, it seemed, about his children. But I came to realise that he found it difficult to praise anyone who was alive (except for Perlemuter), and that there was a bleakness in this, a refusal to give people what they needed, because he had learned to do without what *he* needed. Doing without what he needed became a way of life, with the built-in satisfactions of a martyrdom that never compensated for what he denied himself. Most of his presents to us were given and received in some sense as a reproof: records of Saint-Saëns and (much worse) Sibelius, because he knew I didn't like them and should learn to, and a Czech grammar for my fiftieth birthday, which he may genuinely have imagined would come in handy.

He once thanked my husband for giving him a copy of a book he had just written: it was, my father said, 'one of those books that should be read in very small doses over an extremely long period of time'. No more than the truth, he probably thought, and in tune with how he read books most of the time, anyway; but also characteristically deaf to the dampening impact of his remark. We grew up believing that there was nothing much worse in the world than boasting, exaggeration, flattery, flannel. Only now do I see such precepts as limiting in the way that all style masquerading as morality may be limiting. Indeed, my father appeared to derive some pleasure from the thought that he would never be caught favouring a child of his, and I have since learned that in Japan it is good manners to disparage your own children. I have sometimes wondered whether he felt his own childhood precosity was harmful, luring him into impossible ambitions, and whether he was warning us against hubris, hoping that we would be more reasonable, more moderate in our hopes for ourselves, than he had once been. It is also clear that he regarded his daughters quite straightforwardly as less talented than himself and that he found some consolation in that. Happiness didn't come into it. I don't think he considered that anyone had any business expecting to be happy; and I suspect he told himself that quite often when he was a young man in Paris, and that because he stuck to it, because he went 'absolutely all out' in putting up with the life he had landed himself with, as he expressed it in another letter to his sister-in-law, he expected other people to do so too.

More than fifty years after he wrote that letter from Paris he wrote another, this time to a famous actor he didn't know, a man who has lent his identity as a gay public figure to a campaign to reform aspects of the law relating to homosexual men and women. It is clear from this man's reply that my father had told him about his life in some detail and had particularly asked him for his opinion about the wisdom of bisexual men marrying. Was there any point, hope, future in it? Already in his late eighties by then, he can't, I presume, have been planning an eleventh-hour divorce. He seems also to have added to his letter, perhaps as an afterthought, something to the effect that he had in fact managed to find quite a lot of happiness in his long life.

Family Names and Dates

The Salamans

Myer Salaman (1835–1896) and his wife **Sarah Solomon** (1844–1931) had fourteen surviving children, of whom **Redcliffe** (1874–1955) was the eighth. He married **Nina Davis** (1877–1925) in 1901. They had six children, one of whom died in childhood. My mother, **Ruth** (1909–2001), was their fifth child and older daughter. Redcliffe married **Gertrude Lowy** in 1926. Ruth's oldest brother, Myer (1902–1994), married **Esther Polianowsky** (1900–1995); and her youngest brother, Raphael, married Esther's younger sister, Miriam. **Ruth Salaman** married **Robert Collet** in 1932. They had three daughters, **Jane, Rachel** and **Naomi**.

The Collets

Joseph Collet (1673–1725) was the older brother of **Samuel Collet** (1682–1773) who was known by later generations as 'the Patriarch'. Apart from Joseph, the Collets I write about are descended from Samuel, whose second son, also called **Joseph** (1709–1785), wrote the letters on education that are discussed here to his sister-in-law, **Sarah Lasswell** (1718–1781). She and her husband **Samuel Collet** (1721–1774), the youngest son of 'the Patriarch', were the grandparents of both **John Dobson** (1778–1827) and his cousin **Eliza Barker** (1787–1872), who married in 1810, and of **Collet Barker** (1784–1831), Eliza's brother, and her sister, **Mary Barker** (1792–1885).

John and Eliza had seven children. The second child and oldest son was **Collet Dobson Collet** (1813–1898), who married **Jane Marshall** (1820–1908) in 1854. **Sophia Dobson Collet** (1822–1894) was John and Eliza's fifth child. Collet and Jane had five children: **Caroline** (b.1855), **Wilfred** (1856–1929), my grandfather, **Harold** (b.1858), **Clara** (1860–1948) and **Edith** (b.1862). **Wilfred** married **Mary Ewins**, and they had three sons, of whom the youngest, **Robert Collet** (1905–1993), was my father.

Notes

Portrait of an Artist

p. 1   I think of 'Metroland' as Evelyn Waugh's invention and I thought of where we lived as Metroland because of this and because we were 'on' the Metropolitan Line.

p. 7   Nina Salaman contributed to what became the standard British edition and translation of the *mahzor* or Festival Prayer Book, which was actually produced by her father, Arthur Davis, and Herbert Adler. She began publishing translations of medieval Hebrew poetry when she was still in her teens.

p. 12   J. H. Badley, the founder of Bedales, always known as 'The Chief', wrote about the bad effects of examinations in his *A Schoolmaster's Testament* in 1937.

p. 14   My grandfather's younger brother, Michel Salaman, had known Augustus and Gwen John at the Slade and remained friends with them until the death of Augustus's first wife, Ida Nettleship, for which Michel seems to have blamed Augustus. The letter marvelling at my parents' capacity to look after me was pointed out to me by my friend Mary Taubman, the Gwen John scholar.

p. 20   Robert Collet wrote for *The Score: A Music Magazine*, edited by William Glock, on several occasions. This article was based on the recitals and master classes given by Perlemuter at the Dartington Summer School in 1958. It was published in the November 1958 edition of the magazine.

I should like to thank my cousin Thalia Polak for her help in finding some of the photographs of my mother and for the one of her mother, Esther Salaman, on p. 240.

The Potato Man

In addition to his books, papers and articles and to family letters in my possession, I have consulted the Redcliffe Nathan Salaman Papers in Cambridge University Library. This contains, among much else, the draft of an unpublished autobiography. I have also been greatly helped by discussions with my cousin Nina Wedderburn, with my aunts, Esther Salaman Hamburger and Miriam Salaman, and with Todd Endelman, who is the author of *The Jews of Georgian England, 1714–1830*, and *Radical Assimilation in English Jewish History, 1656–1945,* as well as of articles about both Redcliffe and Nina.

p. 32   James Parkes wrote several books. Two of the best known of these are *A History of the Jewish*

People and *The Foundations of Judaism and Christianity.*

p. 45   A. J. P. Taylor, *English History 1914–1945* (1965). See footnote on p. 98: 'This was the Balfour declaration (8 Nov. 1917). Palestine was at this time inhabited predominantly by Arabs, a fact which the British government brushed lightly aside. Apparently it was assumed that the Arabs would gladly abandon Palestine to the Jews in gratitude for receiving some sort of national existence in the other Ottoman territories. Or maybe Lloyd George and Balfour merely took their knowledge of Palestine from the Bible, which in this respect happened to be out of date. Of course, one purpose of the Balfour declaration was to put a barrier between the French in Syria and the Suez Canal. This was an aspect not aired in public.' Taylor's claim that he had never written books, only chapters, has always impressed me. He was a dab hand at footnotes too.

p. 49   Redcliffe's 'Palestine letters' were reprinted and serialised in 1934–5 by the *Jewish Ex-Serviceman.* When he gave them permission to do so, he insisted that they remove passages containing hostile remarks he had made about the local Arab population, and they agreed to do this.

Three Sisters

p. 71   Perhaps my father was right to play down our

sisterly rivalries, though it didn't always work. My youngest sister once wrote in her diary, 'I must remember to hate R.'

It's a Girl!

p. 79   *Julia, A Portrait of Julia Strachey* by Herself and Frances Partridge was first published by Gollancz in 1983.

J. H. Badley wrote about co-education ad nauseam and with no great conviction or insight, in my view. Nothing he wrote persuades me that he genuinely believed girls and boys should be taught together. Bedales began as a boys' school. Girls were somewhat thrust upon Badley by staff and parents needing a school for their daughters. In Badley's books and articles there is more about 'the difficulties' than the advantages of co-education, and his faith in the efficacy of nude bathing seems born of desperation and is certainly remote from my own experience. I remember a row of little boys, each with an eye glued to the hole in the fence provided by the wood's missing 'knot', watching the girls swimming their lengths. And Badley's reassurances that boys need not become 'effeminate' in co-educational schools, or girls 'hoydenish', read more like warnings than proofs of anything much. It was commonly believed and said for many years that co-education was fine for girls, less fine for boys!

p. 102   Freud once said to Marie Bonaparte, 'The

great question that has never been answered and which I have not yet been able to answer despite my thirty years of research into the feminine soul, is "*Was will das Weib?* [What does Woman want?]"'

Miss Collet

Clara turned herself into the family archivist, and most of what she wrote and collected is now in my possession or in that of my son, Sam Miller. I want to thank him for putting it in order and directing my reading in it. I would also like to thank Dina Copelman for her help in organising sections of this archive and for showing me her work on Clara's stories. Thanks too to Clive Hill for showing me the bibliography he has compiled of Clara's writings and his as yet unpublished 'A Modern Woman's Knowledge: The Empirical Researches of Clara Collet, 1888–1902'. The material relating specifically to Clara consists of diaries, letters, notebooks and three short stories, in addition to her book *Educated Working Women*, which was published by P. S. King in 1902, chapters in Charles Booth's vast project on London and other articles and reports. My father placed copies of a small amount of unpublished material in the Modern Records Centre of the University of Warwick Library, and Clara herself placed copies of some of the family archive in the British Library. I have written about Clara before. This chapter and parts of the next represent a rethinking and reworking of my earlier writing about her. Changes are partly the result of finding new material, though also of writing about her in the context of family relations rather than of feminism and education.

p. 110   Hilda Martindale, *Women Servants of the State 1870–1938. A History of Women in the Civil Service* (1938).

p. 117   Yvonne Kapp writes interestingly about Lissagaray in her biography of Eleanor Marx. His apparent lack of a first name must have been the result of wanting to forget the one he had: Hyppolite-Prosper-Olivier. Kapp regards this nine-year engagement and its ending, brought about by Eleanor, as having damaged her and been partly responsible for her early breakdowns.

p. 124   Ernest Gimson became well known as an architect and furniture designer, responsible, among other things, for the library and the hall at Bedales. Clara later arranged for Gissing's son, Walter, to work with Gimson.

p. 125   Frances Mary Buss, the first woman member of the Council of the College of Preceptors, persuaded them to start training classes for graduates in 1870.

p. 142   I am grateful to Pierre Coustillas, the Gissing scholar, for showing me letters Clara wrote to Morley Roberts between 1904 and 1912.

Taxes on Knowledge

This chapter makes use of Clara's archive: family letters going back to about 1700, Clara's transcriptions of some of the letters and her notes on the family's history. In addition to the privately published book and pamphlet listed below, I have made use of another pamphlet, edited and privately published by Clara, called *Letters of Dr John Collet of Newbury to his brother Joseph*. Clara was involved in the publication by Longmans in 1933 of *The Private Letter Books of Joseph Collet. Sometime Governor of Fort St. George, Madras*, which was edited with an introduction and notes by H. H. Dodwell. She contributed a 40-page history of the Collet family.

I have also made use of Collet Dobson Collet's *History of The Taxes on Knowledge. Their Origin and Repeal*, 2 vols, published in 1899 by T. Fisher Unwin, and of Sophia Collet Dobson's *The Life and Letters of Raja Rammohun Roy*, privately published by Harold Collet in 1900 and reissued with additional material (including a short biography of Sophia) by Hem Chandra Sarkar in Calcutta in 1913.

p. 153   When Harold supposes Clara will one day be the headmistress of a 'public' school, I imagine he means an independent girls' school.

p. 154   John Mulvaney and Neville Green, Australian academics, have recently deciphered and published Collet Barker's journals, for what they reveal about his early 'achievement in race relations' and the texture of life in the frontier settlements in Australia. Their book, published in 1992 by the Melbourne University Press, is called *Commandant of Solitude: The Journals of Captain Collet Barker 1828–1831*.

p. 156   The meeting in Cold Bath Fields presumably

refs to the public protest against the conviction of James Watson for blasphemy in 1832
and his sentence to one year in Cold Bath
Fields prison. Watson became the publisher of
the unstamped Chartist newspaper, the *Working
Man's Friend*.

p. 159 Richard Cobden (1804–1865) was an MP and
Anti-Corn-Law campaigner.

p. 163 These memories of Sunny Bank are Clara's,
written by hand in 1944 and unpublished –
as are her memories of Karl Marx (see below)
– and passed on to me by Dina Copelman.

p. 164 There are copies of the *Free Press* and the
Diplomatic Review in the Newspaper section of
the British Library in Colindale.

p. 168 Clara's memories of Marx were written in
response to a request from Piero Sraffa, who
was in charge of the Marshall Library in the
Economics Faculty at Cambridge in the
1940s.

p. 169 In her long survey article 'Women's Work' for
Charles Booth's *Labour and Life of the People.
Volume 1: East London*, published in 1889, Clara
writes of 'laundresses' as fairly well paid. She
tells us there that the best-paid ironers could
earn as much as 4s or 5s a day.

p. 173 Dante's hostility to the papacy is well known,

though it comes as an interesting surprise to Mary.

p. 175–6   Sophy wrote both these passages in what she called 'An Intellectual Diary' in 1857.

p. 184   These examples of old Samuel's advice to his son Joseph come from the pamphlet Clara had privately printed called *William Whiston's Disciples: In correspondence with each other 1723–1768*.

Samuel Collet's *A Treatise of the Future Restoration of the Jews and Israelites to their own Land* is in the British Library.

p. 185   James Fordyce's *Sermons to Young Women* was published in 1765.

p. 186   William Bowles was a poet Coleridge particularly admired in his youth. His *Fourteen Sonnets* was published in 1789.

Scientific Dialogues. Intended for the Instruction and Entertainment of Young People: in which the first principles of Natural and Experimental Philosophy are fully explained. These were written by the Revd Jeremiah Joyce (1763–1816). John is probably referring here to a second edition of seven volumes, published between 1803 and 1809. Joyce was, incidentally, secretary to the Unitarian Society for many years and tutor to the sons of Lord Stanhope, to whom the books are dedicated. Each volume was devoted to one or a pair of topics: mechanics, astronomy, and so on, and each had a few pages of engravings, mostly diagrams, at the end, and on the title page a quotation from Richard Lovell Edgeworth's *Practical Education* (almost certainly written with his daughter Maria): 'Conversation, with the habit of explaining the meaning of words, and the structure of common domestic implements to children, is the sure and effectual method of preparing the mind for the acquirement of science.'

p. 191   Mary, the great-niece of the author of these letters, endorsed *her* great-niece, Clara's, account of their provenance on the front page of the manuscript in 1878, when she was nearly ninety, and added the words: 'very much the principles on which *we* were trained'. Clara sent her transcription of these letters to my father a month before I was born.

p. 194   Rosalind Mitchison's 'The Numbers Game' in the *New Review* 4:47 (1978). This was a review of Peter Laslett's *Family Life and Illicit Love in Earlier Generations*, and of Lawrence Stone's *The Family, Sex and Marriage in England 1500–1800*.

p. 195   Clara wrote with some passion about how she thought working-class girls should be educated in the chapters she contributed to Booth's *Labour and Life of the People*. Her proposals were practical and geared to the realities of their future lives and work. However, there was an important place for literature: 'education can best be obtained through the medium of good literature. If these children are backward in everything else, in a knowledge of all that is termed "life" they are only too precocious. They know evil so well in too many cases that in offering them of the tree of knowledge we are but introducing them to the good and helping them to discern it. We need not fear to put into their hands, or to give them the key to the works of the great novelists and essayists whom we have recognised as our greatest teachers and our best friends.'

p.196   This passage comes at the end of her book *Educated Working Women*.

This short story by Clara is called 'A Problem for High Schools'.

Outside and In

p. 201   Clara wrote this description of the Collet family in a paper called 'The Private Letter Books of Joseph Collet, sometime Governor of Fort St George, Madras 1717–1720', which was delivered (I think by someone else in her absence) at the Sixth Meeting of the Indian Historical Records Commission held in Madras in January 1924.

p. 212   Joseph also explained to his daughter that he

could not keep Flora himself because of the scandal it would cause.

Happiness

p. 217   My father's translation of Goethe's words was certainly no match for Louis MacNeice's, particularly his version of the 'All that is past of us' poem, which was used in a BBC performance of the symphony in 1949. The *Faust Symphony* combined the music of my father's favourite composer with the ideas and characters of Goethe's play, a work he returned to constantly throughout his life.

p. 238   This comes from the article in *The Score* mentioned in the note for p. 20.

p. 239   Esther Salaman's novels were *Two Silver Roubles* and *The Fertile Plain*. She wrote two books about memory and literature: *A Collection of Moments* and *The Great Confession*.

List of Illustrations

Relations

Acknowledgements

Versions of some of these chapters have appeared in the American quarterly journal, *Raritan*, and I want to thank Richard Poirier for encouraging me to write them in the first place and Jackson Lears and Stephanie Volmer for their fine editorial care. I have relied on the judgement and the enthusiasm of my husband, Karl Miller, in more ways than I can list. I have also been lucky with my other readers so far, and I want to thank them all, especially Emma Tennant and Francis Wyndham, who were early and inspiring ones. I have had help and good advice from Deanne and Joe Bogdan, Dina Copelman, Todd Endelman, Alice Hiller, Joan Scanlon, Imogen Sutton, Jane Taubman and Anne Turvey, and from Daniel, Sam and Georgia Miller as well as Ardashir and Shireen Vakil. I have needed information and letters and photographs and memories, and I am particularly grateful to Rachel and Jonathan Miller and Naomi Roberts, and to Thalia Polak, Nina Wedderburn, Esther and Miriam Salaman and the late Tamara Wordsworth for supplying me with them. I should also like to thank Leo Bersani for permission to quote from his book *Homos*; the British Library for letting me use the photograph of George Gissing; the National Portrait Gallery for the photograph of the Joseph Collet figure, which is now in their possession; and Yvonne Andrews for her photograph of Joseph Miller. Finally, it is a pleasure to be published by Jonathan Cape, for whom I worked as a reader and editor in an earlier life. Thanks to Dan Franklin for his unflagging interest in the project and his friendliness and efficiency and thanks to Alex Butler for her help with the text.

Index